TEACHING
Essential
MATHEMATICS
Grades K-8

To all of my former students:

You were the reason I came to work each day—making a sometimes lonely journey so much brighter with your energy, your humor, and your humanity.

I may not have always liked teaching, but I always loved it. Thank you for all of the great times and special memories.

TEACHING *Essential* MATHEMATICS

Grades K-8

Increasing Engagement and Building Understanding of Key Concepts

Timothy J. McNamara

CORWIN PRESS
A SAGE Company
Thousand Oaks, CA 91320

For information:

Corwin Press
A SAGE Company
2455 Teller Road
Thousand Oaks, California 91320
www.corwinpress.com

SAGE India Pvt. Ltd.
B 1/I 1 Mohan Cooperative Industrial Area
Mathura Road, New Delhi 110 044
India

SAGE Ltd.
1 Oliver's Yard
55 City Road
London EC1Y 1SP
United Kingdom

SAGE Asia-Pacific Pte. Ltd.
33 Pekin Street #02-01
Far East Square
Singapore 048763

Printed in the United States of America.

Library of Congress Cataloging-in-Publication Data

McNamara, Timothy J.
Teaching essential mathematics, grades K-8 : increasing engagement
and building understanding of key concepts / Timothy McNamara.
        p. cm.
Includes bibliographical references and index.
ISBN 978-1-4129-4187-7 (cloth)
ISBN 978-1-4129-4188-4 (pbk.)
    1. Mathematics—Study and teaching (Elementary)—United States.
2. Effective teaching—United States. I. Title.

QA135.6.M396 2008
372.7—dc22   2007026279

This book is printed on acid-free paper.

07   08   09   10   11   10   9   8   7   6   5   4   3   2   1

Acquisitions Editor:	Cathy Hernandez
Editorial Assistants:	Megan Bedell and Cathleen Jane Mortensen
Production Editor:	Nancee McClure
Copy Editor:	Launa Windsor
Typesetter:	C&M Digitals (P) Ltd.
Proofreader:	Caryne Brown
Indexer:	Sheila Bodell
Cover Designer:	Monique Hahn
Graphic Designer:	Lisa Miller

Contents

Preface

When I first began traveling around the country working with teachers in Grades K–12, I thought that every one of my workshop participants came into our sessions with the same love of mathematics that I held.

That assumption was, as the politician might say, not entirely true.

Now, most teachers at the middle and high school levels were hired specifically to teach math, and I hasten to add that the majority of those teachers are comfortable with—no, better yet, even enjoy—teaching it.

However, that is not necessarily the case with the typical self-contained elementary or special education teacher who must wear a variety of hats and give instruction in a much wider range of subjects than just math. While some of those teachers like teaching math, others feel less competent or uncomfortable teaching it.

Truth be told, the single most important determinant for the success of math students at the secondary level is their preparation at the elementary level. But the task today is more daunting than ever, and changes in what is taught, how it should be taught, and especially how much more often it is assessed, impact how elementary teachers feel about teaching mathematics.

So, in response to requests from many outstanding elementary and middle school teachers who have "survived" my workshops, I am offering this collection of creative lessons and activities in order to stimulate the mind and encourage all involved to think differently about math.

Believe me, math is there for the taking. Take a little walk with me and my contributing friends. We think you'll like what you see!

Acknowledgments

Corwin Press gratefully acknowledges the contributions of the following individuals:

Terry Castoria, Seventh-Grade Mathematics Teacher
Marlboro Middle School, Marlboro, NJ

Carrie Chiappetta, Middle School Mathematics Teacher
Scofield Magnet Middle School, Stamford, CT

Joyce Wolfe Dodd, Sixth-Grade Mathematics Teacher
Bryson Middle School, Simpsonville, SC

Debra Rose Howell, Multiage Elementary Teacher
Monte Cristo Elementary School, Granite Falls, WA

Helen Melvin, Second-Grade Teacher
Dr. Levesque Elementary School, Frenchville, ME

Karen Phillips, Eighth-Grade Mathematics and Technology Teacher
Linden Meadows School, Winnipeg, Manitoba, Canada

About the Author

 **Timothy J. McNamara** is a private mathematics consultant specializing in K–12 systemic improvement efforts for schools and school districts nationwide. He is also a consultant for the Mathematics Bureau of the New York State Education Department.

Tim has served as both a math teacher and curriculum supervisor in the western New York State region since 1975. Two of the schools where he has taught—Williamsville East High School near his hometown of Buffalo and Irondequoit High School near Rochester—have been ranked in the top 100 high schools in America by *Newsweek* magazine.

Tim has taught students from Grades 7 through undergraduate, at all levels of ability from remedial to gifted, in both public and private school settings. He also has written articles for math teacher journals from several states and was founder and faculty editor for the Nichols School of Buffalo's student mathematics publication, *The Nth Degree.*

A contributing member for a variety of professional organizations, including the National Council of Teachers of Mathematics, Tim has facilitated countless conference workshops around the country.

Tim was recognized in 1993 when he was honored as the New York State recipient of the prestigious Presidential Award for Excellence in Secondary Mathematics Teaching at ceremonies held in Washington, DC. He also was a state finalist for the same award in 1990 and in 1991.

An accomplished three-sport athlete and coach, Tim was inducted into the Western New York Baseball Hall of Fame in 2002 and had a short appearance as a Pittsburgh Pirate in the 1983 baseball movie, *The Natural,* which starred Robert Redford and was filmed in Buffalo. He is also an avid distance runner, completing four major U.S. marathons in four different cities in the past two years.

He lives in Webster, New York, a suburb of Rochester, with his wife of 28 years, Julie, and they have two children, Jim, 23 (a graduate of Gettysburg (PA) College), and Lucy, 18 (a freshman at Ursinus (PA) College).

Introduction

ANOTHER SWING OF THE PENDULUM?

"Individualized Instruction," "Open Classrooms," "Back-to-Basics." Whether you are a novice teacher or a veteran educator, you are no doubt aware of the "latest things" designed to improve the quality of education for all children across America.

But, as with all trends, they come . . . and they go.

In fact, going back to the mid-1970s, the widely accepted paradigm for schools was called "tracking"—placing students in classrooms depending on their ability. But challenged in the courts as "separate but unequal," tracking has over time given way to "mainstreaming"—placing students in classrooms more randomly, often depending solely on a district's computer placement software.

Ensuring that all students meet high achievement standards is much easier said than done. The levels of ability in a typical classroom today can best be viewed through a theoretical "bell curve" lens—a subset of students who are working at grade level, sandwiched on one side by a subset of students who must work hard to keep up and on the other by a subset of more able students.

And it's the teacher's job to make sure that each child meets standards as represented by statewide assessment—an issue of intense debate, to be sure.

But, unless and until No Child Left Behind becomes an official "latest thing"—and takes its place alongside all of the other trends that have come and gone in the recent history of American education—"it is what it is."

REVERSING THE PLANNING PROCESS

So, does there exist a model for a teacher to create lesson plans that will reach every student, regardless of a disparity in ability levels?

There are two status quo models that more seasoned teachers might recognize. One is "aiming for the middle" of the theoretical bell curve, and the other is (borrowing a term from the 1980s) "trickle down," which aims for the most able students. But, by definition, *neither* planning strategy addresses *every* child's needs.

The thinking behind this book is to start with the least able students in the classroom and expand opportunities for all other students and their levels of ability from there. The needs of *every* child are fully taken into account.

In fact, the theory of multiple intelligences (Gardner, 1993) suggests that everyone uses one or more thought processes—visual/spatial, verbal/ linguistic, and so forth, in addition to logical/mathematical—to internalize information. So, according to this theory, math can be taught in different ways so that a wider representation of students can find their own comfort levels for learning.

My personal experience has been that students enjoy out-of-the-ordinary learning experiences with math, because my simply repeating what the textbook said didn't make my lesson particularly memorable or engaging. I think I also speak for all of my teaching colleagues near and far when I say that, whatever materials might be used, the lesson itself should be inexpensive and allow for quick transitions.

This book is a supplementary resource with lots of hands-on and visual learning experiences for all, with plenty of extension possibilities into areas such as more abstract concepts for the more inquisitive student and graphing calculator applications for every student. There also will be episodes of physical movement and of cooperative learning—all designed to squeeze more discovery and more connections between topics than a textbook is equipped to offer.

The name of the game here is more engagement for more students!

MANY GUIDING HANDS

Writing a book for K–8 teachers turned out to be a more daunting task than I had anticipated. I needed help, and I received it from three excellent sources.

First, I put a call out to fellow winners of the Presidential Awards for Excellence in Science and Mathematics Teaching, and several from the elementary and middle schools took time out of their busy schedules to contribute some of their own personal lessons. A thousand heartfelt "thank you's" go out (in alphabetical order) to Paul Agranoff, Nancy Ann Belsky, Denise Edelson, and Kathy Welch-Martin for their patience with me and their outstanding contributions to this book.

Second, when pulling together pieces that I had accumulated over the years from inservice workshops and conference presentations I had attended and from notes taken from college seminars and professional development publications, I realized that I needed a framework with which to organize my thoughts. So, I returned to an old friend, the National Council of Teachers of Mathematics' (NCTM) *Principles and Standards for School Mathematics* (2000).

The standards defined by NCTM are descriptions of what mathematics instruction should enable all students to know and to do. NCTM has identified ten standards—five content standards (describing the "what") and five process standards (describing the "how")—and most states have adopted these standards into their own curricular documents and grade-level assessments.

This book is presented in a five-chapter format to mirror each of NCTM's five content standards: Numbers and Operations, Algebra, Geometry, Measurement, and Data Analysis and Probability. Within each chapter, student-centered activities are offered that directly align with the various benchmarks that comprise the corresponding standard. This means that you can reference a particular standard and read not only a benchmark for student performance but also a sample idea or interpretation for making that expectation come to life for all of your students.

Third, I've incorporated into these pages some graphing applications/original programs with the TI-73 Explorer model graphing calculator. If you try it, you might like it—and "TI" (Texas Instruments) has some wonderful support mechanisms in place. (Try attending one of their zillion or so yearly T[3] conferences around the country; visit education.ti.com for more information.)

If you do decide to use the TI-73 in any data-intensive classroom applications, keep in mind that any graphing calculator must be "prepared" for a new task. Hence, the highlighted information in the steps below allows you to "clean" your TI-73 of any old material—graphs and data—so as to optimize your chances of technological success:

Using the TI-73: Preparing for New Input/Output

1. Press ON

2. 2nd FORMAT (Select AxesOn)

3. 2nd PLOT 4 ENTER (Shuts off old plots)

4. CLEAR (Go to the Y = screen and CLEAR all old lines)

5. 2nd MEM 6 ENTER CLEAR (Clears all old data)

Your students will learn a great deal from you, and you will not only gain more confidence with the technology every time you use it but also expand your teaching repertoire to attract the more visual learner. It's a classic win-win!

THE SUPPORTING CAST

This book is intended as a resource for newer teachers looking for examples of more inclusive lessons, more experienced teachers wanting to incorporate fresh ideas, supervisors and coordinators searching for models of content review, and pre- and inservice instructors combining math and technology.

Each chapter opens with a two-part introduction—an overview followed by a short tutorial that can be adjusted by the reader into a new classroom activity, or simply considered as a one-to-one discussion. Much like the "cleaning" of the TI-73 graphing calculator just mentioned, the intent of this forum is to prepare the reader to *think* about the mathematics to come—better math teachers are generally better math students.

Every effort was made to make the nearly two dozen activities herein applicable to a wide range of grades; for example, 10 activities can be used at Grade K and 13 activities at Grade 8. They are also fairly inexpensive, quick to implement, interdisciplinary (wherever possible), and sensitive to a wide range of learners in a single classroom setting—hence consistent with an increasingly prevalent differentiated-instruction environment.

To help the reader better determine the appropriateness of each activity, see the following "Activities-by-Grade Chart." The back of the book features two supplemental sections, blackline masters (appendix) and a glossary of terms used, which are also designed to make actually using these activities in the classroom as enjoyable a learning experience as possible.

ACTIVITIES-BY-GRADE CHART

		Grades								
		K	1	2	3	4	5	6	7	8
Chapter 1: Numbers and Operations	MULTFRAX*					X	X	X	X	X
	Double Take	X	X	X	X	X	X	X		
	GCF and LCM					X	X	X	X	X	X
	Make It With an Abacus	X	X	X	X	X	X			
Chapter 2: Algebra	Growing Patterns	X	X	X	X	X	X	X		
	Mathemagic			X	X	X	X	X	X	X
	Divide and Conquer			X	X	X	X	X	X	X
	Raising the Stakes						X	X	X	X
Chapter 3: Geometry	Hands-On Shapes	X	X	X						
	Guess My Pattern	X	X	X	X	X				
	Crazy Quilts		X	X	X	X	X	X		
	Fold It Right There!						X	X	X	X
Chapter 4: Measurement	ACUANGLS*								X	X
	I Scream . . . You Scream . . .					X	X	X		
	How They Stack Up		X	X	X	X	X	X	X	X
	RECTSURA*						X	X	X	X
Chapter 5: Data Analysis and Probability	ODDOREVN*	X	X	X	X	X				
	Read More About It!	X	X	X	X	X	X	X	X	X
	Living Graphs	X	X	X	X	X	X	X		
	Fire and Ice				X	X	X	X	X	X
	Games of Chance	X	X	X	X	X	X	X	X	X

*Original TI-73 program application

Numbers and Operations 1

A high-quality instructional program in Grades K–8 will enable students to:

- Understand numbers, ways of representing numbers, relationships among numbers, and number systems;

- Understand the meanings of operations and how they relate to one another; and

- Compute fluently and make reasonable estimates.

OVERVIEW

The introductory discussion piece, "A Case for 'Why?'" is a manifestation of yours truly's shared constructivist philosophy of teaching math. In plain English, rather than spend all of my time teaching How To (note I said "all" and not "some"—every student needs some amount of time developing a fundamental skill set), I "invest" time in teaching Why.

But why invest in Why? I can think of three good reasons:

1. Why gets to the reasoning behind the concept much faster than How To.

2. How To becomes much easier to teach when Why is explained and reinforced—operations start to "make sense."

3. Students tend to retain the concepts longer, which lessens the amount of time necessary to reteach, reteach, reteach. . . .

So, the piece begins with an example of multiplying two mixed numbers. However, the How To is postponed through a series of visual Why steps: What does a proper fraction mean? What does multiplying two proper fractions look like? What does reducing a fraction both mean and look like? What does a

---

"GCF and LCM" is printed with permission from Paul Arganoff, Mathematics Department Chair, St. Francis Middle School, St. Francis, MN.

"Make It With an Abacus" is printed with permission from Ronald Greaves.

mixed number look like? What does multiplying two mixed numbers (and the resulting equivalent improper fraction) look like?

Only then is How To demonstrated, which then should make more sense than simply performing mindless arithmetic steps without the rationale. An original TI-73 graphing calculator program application (**MULTFRAX**) follows as a means for students to check their written work under adult supervision.

The rest of the chapter contains three activities: "Double Take" uses a standard deck of cards to strengthen arithmetic skills between students, "GCF and LCM" takes a fresh look at the similarities and differences between these two familiar processes, and "Make It With an Abacus" not only helps the student construct but also use a pony-bead abacus with some truly astounding insights into both estimation and precise arithmetic.

A CASE FOR "WHY?"

$$1\tfrac{1}{2} \times 2\tfrac{1}{3} = ?$$

Present this problem to students with the knowledge of how to solve it and access to today's pervasive technology, and the majority of them would first ask, "Where's my calculator?" Then, with TI-73 Explorer graphing calculators in hand, those students would engage the following keys:

1 UNIT 1 (ArrowSouth) 2 (ArrowEast) × 2 UNIT 1 (ArrowSouth) 3 ENTER

And, should the improper fraction $\tfrac{7}{2}$ need to be changed into mixed number form, they would press the button $\mathbf{A\tfrac{b}{c} \leftrightarrow \tfrac{d}{e}}$ to reveal $3\tfrac{1}{2}$.

No doubt the answer is absolutely correct, but what is at stake here? If this and similar mechanical tasks are all that is required for students to demonstrate their "proficiency" in meeting some state-level assessment standard, then we shouldn't be surprised when our country's math students continue to receive mediocre scores on international comparison tests.

Let me hasten to add that yours truly took full advantage of numerous opportunities to apply available technology in my own math classes (to *check* answers, for example). In fact, this book itself features several original programs written for the TI-73.

Moreover, the whole point of this chapter is to discuss how to get the right answer. Agreed! But, if you as the instructor are given time with your students to actually *teach* them, then it is in everyone's best long-term interest that less time be spent on *how* and more time be spent on *why* math is the way it is.

The reader is encouraged to remember four very basic teaching criteria:

Rule 1. Since learning math is an active and accumulative process, it is far more engaging for students to "do" math than just receive it.

Rule 2. Math should *always* make sense. (If it doesn't, a student's ensuing confusion will eventually lead to frustration and a loss of confidence.)

Rule 3. The wider your teaching repertoire, the more students you'll have a chance to reach (aka the "bigger net" theory).

Rule 4. Standing in front of a classroom and reading aloud from the textbook is still reading. Reading is generally *not* teaching (see Rule 1).

So, for our purposes here, what is the thought process that fills in all the "middle stuff"—that is, *why* did we get $3\frac{1}{2}$ as the answer to our original question? Well, there are some who would get out paper and pencil, change the original mixed numbers to improper fractions, and respond this way:

$$\tfrac{3}{2}\times\tfrac{7}{3}=\tfrac{21}{6}=3\tfrac{3}{6}=3\tfrac{1}{2}$$

Still others would pursue more of a "short-cut" strategy:

$$\tfrac{3}{2}\times\tfrac{7}{3}=\tfrac{7}{2}=3\tfrac{1}{2}$$

But the two processes above are strictly algorithmic—as one's textbook might explain, perform step A, then step B, and so forth. So up to now, we have identified *how* to get to $3\frac{1}{2}$ in three ways, but we have yet to determine *why*. We might successfully answer a similar state-level test question, but more than likely we haven't the foggiest notion what's actually going on here.

The explanation that follows takes into account the fact that, contrary to the discrete nature of the chapters of this book, the five paralleling NCTM standards work in conjunction with each other. The search for Why will require us to integrate the more abstract process standards (problem solving, reasoning, communication, connections, and representation).

For example, here we shall revisit the meaning of a fraction (communication) by making some visual models (representation), starting with some easier examples (a problem-solving strategy). When we introduce operations and begin to compare our results (connections), we shall be on our way (reasoning) to understanding.

That understanding should help us explain *why* the steps we took in our earlier algorithmic processes actually worked—*not just how* they worked.

1a. What does $\frac{3}{5}$ mean?

Always think "Bottoms Up!" Taking a whole unit (here we're using a rectangle), first cut it into five fifths (the bottom number, or denominator). Then color in three of those five regions (the top number, or numerator).

But a lot more math than that can be squeezed out of this one model. If, for example, we consider the rectangle to represent $1.00 US, then each of the five regions would represent $\frac{1}{5}$ of that dollar, or $0.20. And, by extension, since the word "percent" literally means "out of 100," each of the 20 cents would be equivalent to 20% of that one dollar (and $20\% \times 5 = 100\%$).

So, the three shaded regions—each of which separately equals $0.20—would altogether represent $3 \times \$0.20$, or = $0.60. What could we do with 60¢?

1b. If I had a friend, I might split my $0.60 "right down the middle," give him half, and keep half for myself. How much money would I now have (Figure 1.1)?

Think about this! Working with money should present little or no problem—half of $0.60 is $0.30 (30¢ for me, 30¢ for my friend). However, students tend to lose their insight when it comes to the same problem—in *fraction form*!

Basically, the words "half of" translate mathematically into " $\frac{1}{2}$ times," or $\frac{1}{2} \times$. So, if we rewrite 0.60 as $\frac{3}{5}$ (of a dollar), then the question becomes:

1c. What does $\frac{1}{2} \times \frac{3}{5}$ look like? (See Figure 1.2 for a model of this operation.)

Thinking "Bottoms Up!," the fraction $\frac{1}{2}$ means two regions (established by the horizontal line), of which we're only interested in one region (the top half shaded with slanted lines in the opposite direction).

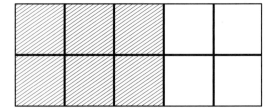

Figure 1.1

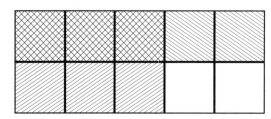

Figure 1.2

Although the answer is much more apparent for students who use two colors (one for $\frac{3}{5}$, the other for $\frac{1}{2}$) the ten regions so displayed contain only three regions that have been colored twice (or, here, have a double-slanted "mesh" design) $=\frac{3}{10}$.

Now the algorithmic process that produces the same answer—the product of the two numerators ($1 \times 3 = 3$) and the product of the two denominators ($2 \times 5 = 10$)—should begin to make more sense:

$$\tfrac{1}{2} \times \tfrac{3}{5} = \tfrac{3}{10}$$

2a. What is $\frac{2}{3} \times \frac{4}{5}$? (Various models related to this question will appear below.) Let's work backwards (another problem-solving strategy), beginning with creating a visual representation of the fraction $\frac{4}{5}$.

Incidentally, the reader may now wish to engage the entire class in the modeling process by passing out to each student 3-by-5 cards, two markers of different colors, a pen or pencil, and a ruler.

(Remember: "Bottoms Up!") Have each student draw four vertical lines one inch apart in order to establish the five regions that make up the denominator "5." Then, taking one of the markers, color in four of the regions to represent the numerator "4" (see Figure 1.3).

Continuing to work and read backwards, next have each student draw two horizontal lines one inch apart in order to establish the three regions that make up the denominator "3" of the other fraction in the problem (Figure 1.4).

Then, taking the other marker, color in one of the horizontal regions to represent the numerator "1" (Figure 1.5). If the question had read, "What is $\frac{1}{3} \times \frac{4}{5}$?" the answer would be the four squares that had been colored twice (or, here, have a double-slanted "mesh" design) $=\frac{4}{15}$.

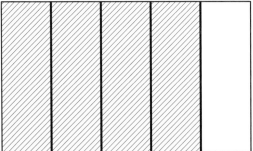

Figure 1.3

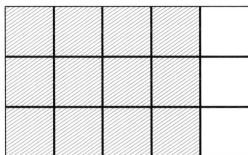

Figure 1.4

We are interested here, however, in modeling and evaluating the question, "What is $\frac{2}{3} \times \frac{4}{5}$?" So, we must color a second horizontal strip as illustrated (Figure 1.6), which means that eight of the fifteen squares are double-colored (or "meshed") $= \frac{8}{15}$.

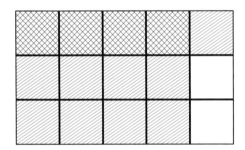

Figure 1.5

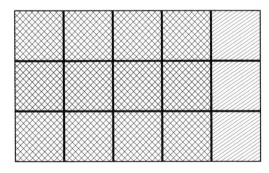

Figure 1.6

The same effect, of course, can be created with the product of the numerators ($2 \times 4 = 8$) and the product of the denominators ($3 \times 5 = 15$). But, let's keep an eye on a developing pattern (another problem-solving strategy):

$$\tfrac{2}{3} \times \tfrac{4}{5} = 2 \times (\tfrac{1}{3} \times \tfrac{4}{5}) = 2 \times (\tfrac{4}{15}) = \tfrac{8}{15}$$

2b. It may appear redundant, but what would $\frac{3}{3} \times \frac{4}{5}$ look like?

Continue by erasing the color from any single-colored square in Figure 1.7 and removing the two horizontal lines (Figure 1.8). Now, doesn't this model look familiar? How would you describe (communicate) what fraction this model represents?

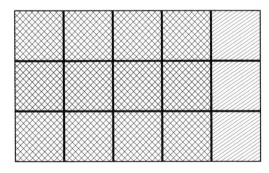

Figure 1.7

Figure 1.8

It would appear that, without bothering to simplify the fraction the more traditional way (in this case, dividing both the numerator and the denominator by 3), $\frac{12}{15} = \frac{4}{5}$. Actually, the visual concept of "simplifying" is akin to the removal of the two horizontal lines in the model!

So, if you know (can you see the model in your head?) that $\frac{3}{3} = 1$, then, because anything times 1 is itself (**multiplicative identity**) (Figure 1.9):

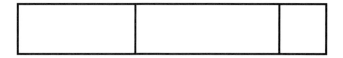

$$\frac{\cancel{3}}{\cancel{3}} \times \frac{4}{5} = 3 \times \left(\frac{1}{3} \times \frac{4}{5}\right) = 3 \times \left(\frac{4}{15}\right) = \frac{12}{15}$$

$$1 \times \frac{4}{5} = \frac{4}{5} \quad \longleftarrow$$

Figure 1.9

3. So, what will $1\frac{1}{2} \times 2\frac{1}{3}$ look like, and how will it help students gain insight? (Various models related to this question will appear below.)

Classroom participation will require a little more preparatory effort on the part of the teacher. Besides the materials mentioned before, each student should also have access to several 2-by-7 copies or cutouts of the model of $2\frac{1}{3}$ (Figure 1.10), along with a pair of safety scissors.

Figure 1.10

We start with $2\frac{1}{3}$ (working backwards as done before), and we should notice how that particular mixed number is depicted—two whole rectangles and a third of another. Our solution strategy begins by thinking of the other mixed number in the problem, $1\frac{1}{2}$, as $\frac{3}{2}$ (an improper fraction) or, more important, as "three halves" when translated into English.

So, take one copy of the model, draw one horizontal line one inch from the top and bottom (Figure 1.11).

Figure 1.11

Label the six regions so created . . . :

A	C	E
B	D	F

Figure 1.12

Concentrate on one of the horizontal halves (for the sake of the diagram in Figure 1.13, the top half—the "odd pieces"—are in focus). . . .

A	C	E

Figure 1.13

Take scissors, cut off and discard the bottom half, cut/detach the odd pieces from each other, and rearrange them into a new (rectangular) whole (Figure 1.14).

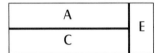

Figure 1.14

Now, regions A and C make up a new "1" (compare it with the "1's" back in the original 2-by-7 model). But the coolest aspect of this entire process is region E, because it turns out that six of our little region E's can fit vertically upon and within the "1" space (combined regions A and C) we just created.

Therefore, region $E = \frac{1}{6}$ making the new configuration equal to $1\frac{1}{6}$ or $\frac{7}{6}$.

Figure 1.15

Recall the question is asking for "three halves" of $2\frac{1}{3}$, which has come to mean that we need to add three of the above configurations (three "1's" and three of the $\frac{1}{6}$ pieces).

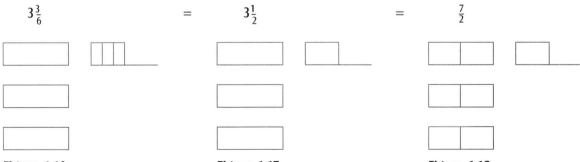

$3\frac{3}{6}$		$=$	$3\frac{1}{2}$		$=$	$\frac{7}{2}$	

Figure 1.16   **Figure 1.17**   **Figure 1.18**

CALCULATOR APPLICATION (GRADES 4–8)

Multiplying Fractions

The original program, MULTFRAX, below will allow the user to check paper-and-pencil answers in multiplying two fractions (either proper or improper).

(Note: The "F ↔ D" portion of the second to last step of the program is the white-colored button on the TI-73's display panel that, when depressed, changes fractional answers to decimals or vice versa.)

For demonstration purposes here, we will be solving $1\frac{1}{2} \times 2\frac{1}{3}$ in improper fraction form—that is, $\frac{3}{2} \times \frac{7}{3} = ?$

PROGRAM:MULTFRAX	:Pause	:Pause
:ClrScreen	:ClrScreen	:ClrScreen
:Disp "FIND_THE_ PRODUCT"	:Disp "FOR_(A/B),"	:Disp "ANSWER_="
:Disp "OF_2_FRAC TIONS"	:Input "A_=_,"A	:Disp "_"
:Disp "OF_THE_FORM"	:Input "_and_B_=_,"B	:Disp (AxC) / (BxD) ->
:Disp "_"	:Disp "_"	F ↔ D
:Disp "(A/B)_x_(C/D)"	:Disp :FOR_(C/D),"	:Pause
	:Input "C_=_,"C	
	:Input "_and_D_=_,"D	

Input

Erase Phase: Clear out all old input from your calculator ("how to" steps appear in the introduction to this book).
PRGM
Scroll down (ArrowSouth)
  to MULTFRAX
ENTER

ENTER

ENTER
3 ENTER
2 ENTER
7 ENTER
3 ENTER

ENTER

ENTER
ENTER (for reset)
or
CLEAR
2nd OFF (for shut down)

Output

prgmMULTFRAX

FIND THE PRODUCT
OF 2 FRACTIONS
OF THE FORM:
(A/B) × (C/D)

FOR (A/B),
A = 3
and B = 2
FOR (C/D),
C = 7
and D = 3

ANSWER =
3 u $\frac{1}{2}$

prgmMULTFRAX
Done

DOUBLE TAKE
(Grades K–6) (Materials: Deck of playing cards, worksheet, pencil)

NCTM Standard: Students will be able to understand numbers, ways of representing numbers, relationships among numbers, and number systems.

There are hosts of stimulating arithmetic activities that can be produced from a standard deck of 52 playing cards. For these first three activities, students are paired off: Student A is designated as the first two-card selector, and Student B is designated the first recorder (turns are alternated).

The teacher moves around the room among the pairings, and Student A in each group takes any two cards ("Pick a card, any card. Now, do it again."). Student A then places the two cards face up, while Student B gets ready to fill in the chart (see blackline masters in appendix) with Student A's responses.

Let's suppose Student A picks the 8 of clubs and the 6 of diamonds. Student B then writes in the first column "8 clubs" in the space next to Card 1 and "6 diamonds" in the space next to Card 2.

Activity 1: Beginning Operations
(Larger Number First for Grades K–3)

Whatever the two selections, the suits in this first activity are ignored. Student A uses the number values of the two cards to perform the operations of addition and subtraction (K possible?) and multiplication (his or her verbal answers are entered in the first column by Student B up to the second horizontal line in the chart). Answers: $8 + 6 = 14$, $8 - 6 = 2$, and $8 \times 6 = 48$.

When a pairing is ready to continue, Student B (turns are alternated) may select the next two cards. Student A takes on the role of recorder (now in the second column), and the activity proceeds as before.

Note: Face cards (Jack, Queen, and King) each have an equivalent value of 10. However, more able students should be challenged by giving each face card its own unique equivalence—Jack = 11, Queen = 12, and King = 13.

Activity 2: Intermediate Operations (Grades 3–6)

Whatever the two selections, the suits in this next activity are still ignored. Recall that the numerical values of the two cards first picked by Student A were 8 and 6. The task ahead is for Student A to answer all of the questions in the first column of the chart.

Since the definition of an **improper fraction** requires that the numerator be larger than the denominator, Student A rearranges the cards from side-by-side (in order of selection) to one on top of the other—in this case, $\frac{8}{6}$.

As recorded by Student B in the first column of the chart: Answers = 14, 2, and 48 (like before); improper fraction = $\frac{8}{6}$, reduced = $\frac{4}{3}$, **proper fraction** (switch the positions of the top and bottom cards) = $\frac{6}{8}$, reduced = $\frac{3}{4}$, decimal (for the proper fraction) = 0.75, percent = 75.

Activity 3: Mastery Operations (Grades 5–6)

In this activity, we begin to distinguish between "black" cards (the suits clubs and spades) and "red" cards (the suits diamonds and hearts). Moreover, black cards now represent **positive integers** and red cards negative integers.

	Student A _____		Student B _____	
	1st Picks A	1st Picks B	2nd Picks A	2nd Picks B
Card #1:	+8			
Card #2:	−6			
Sum:	+2			
Difference:	+14			
Product:	−48			
Improper Fraction:	$-\dfrac{8}{6}$			
Fraction Reduced:	$-\dfrac{4}{3}$			
Mixed Number:	$-1\dfrac{1}{3}$			
Proper Fraction:	$-\dfrac{6}{8}$			
Fraction Reduced:	$-\dfrac{3}{4}$			
Decimal:	−0.75			
Percent:	−75%			

Note: There are two real-life examples of positive black and negative red—in business (when one is "in the black," there is profit) and on the leaderboards at a golf tournament.

Consider the filled-in first column of the chart on the previous page. Student B entered cards 1 and 2 not as before but as (+ 8) and (− 6), respectively. Students will also experience some new wrinkles while formulating answers in this activity because of the presence of integers, especially when subtracting and multiplying or dividing.

As with this or either of the other two activities, the teacher may choose to alter the chart depending on the ability levels of the students. The teacher may also wish to collect the worksheets at the end of the lesson in order to assess for accuracy.

Overhead Transparency Cards Activities

Have one student come to the front of the room, select two overhead transparency playing cards from a deck of yours that you have invested in and own, and display the two chosen cards on an overhead projector. Here are some alternative activities to consider for your class:

1. *Stations*: Students move around the room from the "Multiply" table to the "Decimal" table to the "Improper Fraction" table, etc., all the while writing answers to what they are observing on the overhead.

2. *Team competitions*: The room is divided in half and one student stands at the overhead. That student not only picks the cards but also spins an overhead spinner—a transparent version with sections that can be prelabeled (Add, Subtract, etc.) according to ability level. Contestants must use the two chosen playing cards and the direction from the just-spun spinner to try to guess the correct answer (the teacher keeps score and/or moderates).

3. *Buzz*: Similar to Team Competitions above in that one student chooses the cards and the operation, and the rest of the class form a line along the side of the room and answer rapid-fire questions while on their feet.

A One-On-One Activity: "Salute"

Two students face each other, and each picks one card from a face down standard deck *without* looking at their own cards (kept face down).

On the signal from the teacher, the students then raise their respective cards to their foreheads and—much like the traditional British method of palm-out saluting—show the other person their card (again, *without* ever looking at their own card).

Let's suppose Student A has the 4 of hearts (or −4) and Student B has the 5 of spades (or +5). The teacher then states an operation and a value. For example, the teacher might say, "Addition, +1."

Given first turn, Student A—seeing Student B's +5—tries to identify her *own* card and (hopefully) says either 4 of hearts or 4 of diamonds.

GCF AND LCM

Guest Contributor: Paul Agranoff

(Grades 3–8) (Materials: Worksheet, paper, and pencil)

NCTM Standard: Students will be able to understand meanings of operations and how they relate to one another.

Many students struggle with the concepts of **greatest common factor** (GCF) and **least common multiple** (LCM). When they hear of these two number theory concepts, their lack of understanding frequently causes them to confuse the two ideas and misidentify them.

The following is a different approach to understanding the difference between the GCF and LCM concepts. It also integrates other number theory ideas: prime and composite numbers, prime factorization and divisibility patterns, and common factors.

Prime and Composite Numbers

Traditionally, the technique of "decomposing" numbers is performed by using factor trees. An alternative approach to this method is prime factorization via prime number divisibility. Instruction begins with students completing the *Sieve of Eratosthenes.*

This activity "sifts out" all of the prime numbers less than 50 (or 100, if you prefer) and helps students develop a sense of prime and composite numbers. Before you begin, supply your students with a copy of the number table (found as a blackline master in appendix).

Then, complete the next six steps to determine the prime and composite numbers less than or equal to 50.

1	2	3	4	5	6	7	8	9	10
11	12	13	14	15	16	17	18	19	20
21	22	23	24	25	26	27	28	29	30
31	32	33	34	35	36	37	38	39	40
41	42	43	44	45	46	47	48	49	50

Figure 1.19

Step 1: Cross out the number 1 in the chart (Figure 1.19). The number 1 is neither **prime** (only divisible by itself and 1) nor **composite** (a product of at least two primes), but it is a factor of every number.

1	②	3	4	5	6	7	8	9	10
11	12	13	14	15	16	17	18	19	20
21	22	23	24	25	26	27	28	29	30
31	32	33	34	35	36	37	38	39	40
41	42	43	44	45	46	47	48	49	50

Figure 1.20

Step 2: Circle the number 2 (Figure 1.20). Not only is it the first prime number, but it is also the only prime that is even. Then cross out all the multiples of 2, which would all be even. (Are there patterns in the chart? If you see one, describe it.)

1	②	③	4	5	6	7	8	9	10
11	12	13	14	15	16	17	18	19	20
21	22	23	24	25	26	27	28	29	30
31	32	33	34	35	36	37	38	39	40
41	42	43	44	45	46	47	48	49	50

Figure 1.21

Step 3: Circle the number 3 (Figure 1.21). Then cross out all the remaining multiples of 3 (single slash marks). (Are there new patterns in the chart? If you see one, describe it.) (Hint: Do you play chess?)

1	②	③	4	⑤	6	7	8	9	10
11	12	13	14	15	16	17	18	19	20
21	22	23	24	25	26	27	28	29	30
31	32	33	34	35	36	37	38	39	40
41	42	43	44	45	46	47	48	49	50

Figure 1.22

Step 4: Circle the number 5 (Figure 1.22), and cross out the two remaining multiples of 5 (single slashes). (Again, are there any patterns in the chart worth mentioning?)

Step 5: Circle the number 7 (Figure 1.23)—the next prime number—and its remaining multiple (and guess what that number is before you look for it in the chart).

1̶	②	③	4̶	⑤	6̶	⑦	8̶	9̶	1̶0̶
11	1̶2̶	13	1̶4̶	1̶5̶	1̶6̶	17	1̶8̶	19	2̶0̶
2̶1̶	2̶2̶	23	2̶4̶	2̶5̶	2̶6̶	2̶7̶	2̶8̶	29	3̶0̶
31	3̶2̶	3̶3̶	3̶4̶	3̶5̶	3̶6̶	37	3̶8̶	3̶9̶	4̶0̶
41	4̶2̶	43	4̶4̶	4̶5̶	4̶6̶	47	4̶8̶	4̶9̶	5̶0̶

Figure 1.23

Step 6: Circle all of the remaining numbers (Figure 1.24). (These are all of the prime numbers less than or equal to 50.)

1̶	②	③	4̶	⑤	6̶	⑦	8̶	9̶	1̶0̶
⑪	1̶2̶	⑬	1̶4̶	1̶5̶	1̶6̶	⑰	1̶8̶	⑲	2̶0̶
㉑	2̶2̶	㉓	2̶4̶	2̶5̶	2̶6̶	2̶7̶	2̶8̶	㉙	3̶0̶
㉛	3̶2̶	3̶3̶	3̶4̶	3̶5̶	3̶6̶	㊲	3̶8̶	3̶9̶	4̶0̶
㊶	4̶2̶	㊸	4̶4̶	4̶5̶	4̶6̶	㊼	4̶8̶	4̶9̶	5̶0̶

Figure 1.24

Prime Factorization by Divisibility

Rather than use factor trees, divisibility patterns (a "ladder" format) can be used to decompose composite numbers into their prime factors. For example, let's decompose the composite number 72 (Figure 1.25):

First, is 72 even? Yes, all even numbers are divisible by 2.
Is 36 even? Yes, all even numbers are divisible by 2.
Is 18 even? Yes, all even numbers are divisible by 2.
Is 9 even? No, but it is divisible by the next prime number, 3.
Is 3 even? No, but it is divisible by 3.

```
2 | 72
2 | 36
2 | 18
3 |  9
3 |  3
        1
```

Figure 1.25

When we reach a value of 1, the composite number has been decomposed into its prime factors. The **prime factorization** of any number is the product of its divisors ($2 \times 2 \times 2 \times 3 \times 3 = 72$).

In fact, it turns out that composite numbers can be decomposed into their prime factors using the same technique and some basic rules of divisibility:

Divisible by 2 if the last digit of the given number is even
Divisible by 3 if the *sum* of the digits of the given number makes a new number that is divisible by 3
Divisible by 5 if the last digit of the given number is a 5 or a 0

The next prime factors (7, 11, 13, etc.) may on occasion need to be used.

Greatest Common Factor (GCF)

With the same technique as for prime factorization, two or more numbers can be decomposed simultaneously (Figure 1.26). When the prime factors that are used to decompose the two or more numbers are multiplied, the product is the GCF:

Both numbers are even: divide by 2 (common prime factor).
Both numbers are still even: repeat the process.
Two is no longer a common factor, but 3 is: divide both by 3.
There are no more common factors: process complete.

```
2 | 36  84
2 | 18  42
3 |  9  21
        3   7
```

Figure 1.26

Common
Factors

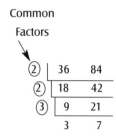

Figure 1.27

Since there are no more common factors, the numbers 3 and 7 are said to be "**relatively prime**." We can now state that the GCF of 36 and 84 is the product of the divisors/common prime factors (circled numbers in the figure below) = $2 \times 2 \times 3 = 12$.

In addition, we have modeled the decomposing of common factors used in simplifying fractions (Figure 1.27). Note that dividing both the numerator and denominator of the fraction $\frac{36}{84}$ by the GCF of 12 gives you $\frac{3}{7}$ —the simplified version of $\frac{36}{84}$ *in lowest terms*.

Least Common Multiple (LCM)

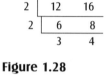

Figure 1.28

With the same technique as for the GCF, we can determine the LCM of two or more numbers. The GCF value on the left side of the process gives us the common factors. The relatively prime values at the bottom give us the uncommon prime factors. The product of the common and the uncommon factors of two or more numbers is the LCM, as shown in the following new example (Figure 1.28):

Both numbers are even: divide them by 2.
Both numbers are still even: repeat the process.
There are no more common factors: process complete.

Common
Factors

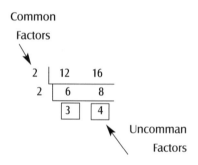

Uncomman
Factors

Figure 1.29

Since the numbers 3 and 4 are relatively prime, we can now state that the LCM of 12 and 16 is the product of the common factors and the uncommon factors: $2 \times 2 \times 3 \times 4 = 48$ (Figure 1.29).

(Think of an imaginary "L" going down (2×2) and then under (3×4) the entire figure. "L" stands for "Least.")

Contrasting the GCF and LCM

By using this technique after becoming more confident with finding prime numbers (the Sieve), students should recognize the difference between the GCF (the product of common factors vertically arranged on the left side) and the LCM (the product of the common *and* uncommon factors which are located along the bottom).

As you are well aware, both of these concepts are critical to a student's future success with fractional operations. The GCF is an important component in simplifying fractions, and the LCM plays a similar role with adding and subtracting fractions with unlike denominators (the LCM becomes the LCD).

Guest contributor Paul Agranoff, mathematics department chair, St. Francis Middle School, St. Francis, MN, has spent thirty years in middle-level education as a classroom teacher and department chair. He was the 1993 Minnesota recipient of the Presidential Award for Excellence in Elementary Mathematics Teaching while a sixth-grade teacher.

MAKE IT WITH AN ABACUS

(Grades K–5) (Materials: Listed below)

NCTM Standard: Students will be able to compute fluently and to make reasonable estimates.

This hands-on activity allows students to make their own calculating device (an abacus) and then use it to solve one- and two-digit addition, subtraction, and multiplication problems. It is the brainchild of the author's former colleague in the West Irondequoit Central School District north of Rochester, NY, retired K–12 science supervisor Ronald Greaves, and its attraction rests with the variety of tactile, sensory, and mathematical intelligence therein.

As the title of this piece suggests, there are two distinct phases to this learning activity for the student—the "assemble" phase (actually building a very inexpensive abacus), and the "calculate" phase (using that abacus to become more proficient and more confident in performing simple computations).

An **abacus** is defined as "a manual computing device consisting of a frame holding parallel rods strung with movable counters." In order for students to make their own rudimentary versions, the teacher should have the following:

1. Two prepunched tongue depressors (about 14 cm in length)
2. Five 11 cm-long dowel segments ($\frac{1}{8}$" diameter)
3. Fifty pony beads in five different colors (10 beads × 5 colors)
4. A small tube of school glue
5. A small roll of transparent tape (if necessary)
6. Some paper towels (for cleanup)

The teacher must ready the first two items on the materials list in advance, but the other four can be provisioned for the entire class. The teacher for early elementary (K and 1) grades should already have on hand several preconstructed abaci to distribute to the class.

Preparation: For a class of 25 students, the teacher will need to pre-punch at least 50 tongue depressors (2 per student—Popsicle sticks don't seem to work as well). Holes of $\frac{1}{8}$" diameter should be prepunched (reading left to right and in the middle of each stick) at these intervals: 2cm, 4.5 cm, 7 cm, 9.5 cm, and 12 cm.

The dowel segments are to be cut from $\frac{1}{8}$" × 48" craft wood dowels (available at most hardware outlets). Each 48" dowel will yield 11 segments that are 11 cm in length, which means that, since 125 segments are needed for a 25-student class (25 × 5 segments per student), at least 12 dowels need to be measured out and precut.

Cost: Items a teacher must always have are a revolving punch ($5–$10) and a pair of straight-cut snips ($10, unless he or she already has a pair for trimming garden plants).

Materials requiring constant replenishment: tongue depressors (a box of 100 sells for $5 at a specialty pharmacy), dowels (twenty-five 48" lengths sell for $5), and pony beads (a bag of 250 to 300 sells for $3 at a fabric or craft outlet. One class will easily go through 5 bags, so have some backups ready just in case).

Items such as glue, tape, and towels may already be on site.

Cost per student:
Two tongue depressors (5¢ apiece) = $0.10
Five dowel segments ($\frac{1}{2}$ dowel @ 20¢ apiece) = $0.10
Fifty beads ($\frac{1}{5}$ of a $3 bag) = $0.60
Incidentals (glue, tape, paper towels) = $0.20
Sum total cost per student = about $1.00

Steps in construction: Once each student has all of the materials together, it's time to build an abacus (about 20–30 min.).

How to Assemble

Step 1: Take all five of the dowel segments (the thinner vertical lines in Figure 1.30) and string 10 beads of the same color through each one.

Step 2: Fit each dowel segment through holes in the prepunched tongue depressors (the thicker horizontal lines), and add a small dab of glue at each juncture.

Step 3: Level off the ends of the dowel segments top and bottom (about 1.5 cm should protrude for each piece). Use paper towels for cleanup or to wipe away excess glue. The glue should take about 5 to 10 minutes to set, and then the abacus should be checked for any cracks in the tongue depressors (use a bit of tape for repairs as necessary).

How to Calculate

With apologies to any readers who have been taught otherwise, using our 10-bead abacus here requires resting it flat on a desk (Figure 1.30) and sliding all of the beads to the top tongue depressor (Figure 1.31). Those beads on the far right dowel segment are the units numbers, those to its left (second from the right) are the tens numbers, and so forth.

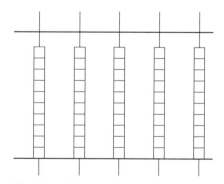

Figure 1.30

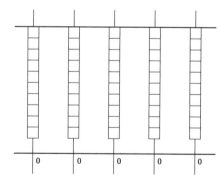

Figure 1.31

Note: Numbers have been superimposed along the bottom of the figure so that the reader may better follow the six examples that follow.

1. Simple addition: 2 + 5

Take a sharp pencil and slide the first two beads down on the units bar (as shown in Figure 1.32).

Then, from that "2 space" you just created on the units bar, count up five more beads and slide them down on top of the other two (note the new "7 space" created in Figure 1.33).

Answer: 2 + 5 = 7

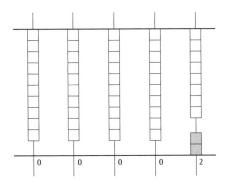

Figure 1.32

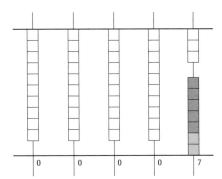

Figure 1.33

2a. Addition with "carrying" (Method 1): 8 + 9

Take a sharp pencil and slide the first eight beads down on the units bar (Figure 1.34).

If you try to slide 9 additional beads down on the units bar, you have a problem—there are only 2 left! So, slide the 2 beads down that you have available (which makes 10, as indicated in Figure 1.35).

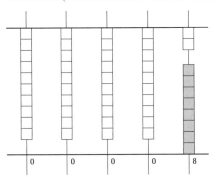

Figure 1.34

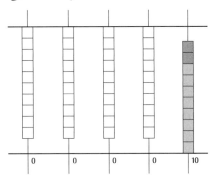

Figure 1.35

Make the equivalent version of that 10 (slide all the units beads back up and slide one tens bead down), as in Figure 1.36.

Remember that you wanted to add 9 but have already used 2 of the 9 units beads. Since 9 − 2 = 7, go back to the units bar and slide down the remaining 7 beads you need (as indicated in Figure 1.37).

Answer: 8 + 9 = 17

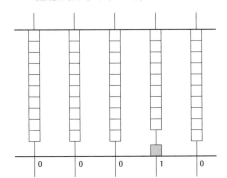

Figure 1.36

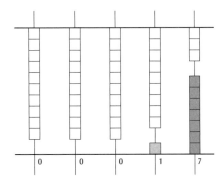

Figure 1.37

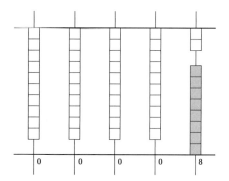

Figure 1.38

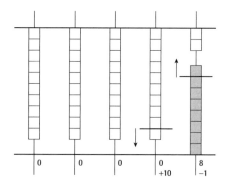

Figure 1.39

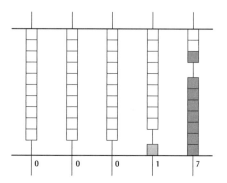

Figure 1.40

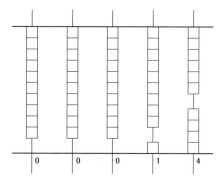

Figure 1.41

2b. Addition with "give and take" (Method 2): 8 + 9

Same problem: take a sharp pencil and slide the first eight beads down on the units bar (Figure 1.38).

At this point and for the purpose of reinforcing a key concept, the reader is directed back to part of the NCTM Standard statement at the beginning of this piece: "to compute fluently and to make reasonable estimates."

It is important for the student to understand the concept of "closeness"—in this case, *how close* is 9 to 10? If your students agree that 9 is 1 away from 10, then the class is free to discover one of the treasures of the abacus (and why it is such a great computing device for everyone).

Think of adding 9 (Figure 1.39) as actually doing two things:

"Taking" a 10 (plus) (a tens bead slides down)

and

"Giving back" a 1 (minus) (a units bead slides back up)

The result is:
$$8 + 9 = 8 + (10 - 1)$$
$$= 8 + 10 - 1$$
$$= (8 + 10) - 1$$
$$= 18 - 1$$
$$= 17 \text{ (Figure 1.40)}$$

Author's aside: Perhaps our drive in this country to teach students the best way, only way approach to the right answer (and fortified with pencil-and-paper seatwork) may neglect an opportunity for us and for our students to apply estimation skills. This may explain in part why students in other countries tend to think more globally at a much earlier age.

3. Subtraction (no "borrowing"): 14 − 8

Take a sharp pencil and slide the first bead down on the tens bar and the first four beads down on the units bar (Figure 1.41).

Recall that we just added 9 as 10 − 1. By the "give-and-take" process, we "took" 10 (slid a tens bead down) and "gave" a 1 (slid a units bead up). If students get confused, it helps to remember this phrase: *Take Down or Give Up.*

Now we shall be subtracting as a reverse process of adding:

$$14 - 8 = 14 - (10 - 2) = 14 - 10 + 2$$

So, reversing our previous moves (see Figure 1.42), we are going to "give" 10 (slide a tens bead up) and "take" 2 (slide two units beads down).

Answer: 14 − 8 = 6

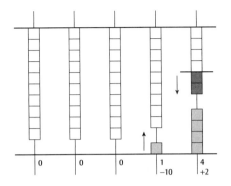

Figure 1.42

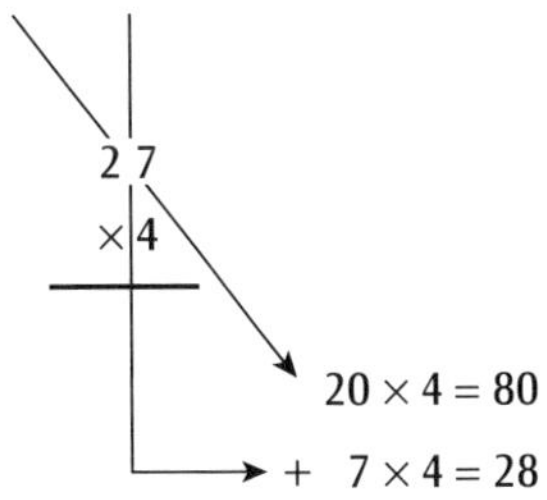

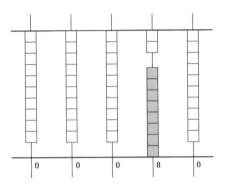

Figure 1.43

4a. Two-digit by one-digit multiplication: 27×4 (left to right)

Follow the arrows in Figure 1.43. First, multiply 2×4, which is actually 20×4 (think 2×4 with a zero tacked on the end) or 80 (Figure 1.44).

Next, multiply 7×4 and add the product 28 to the 80 already on the abacus (Figure 1.45).

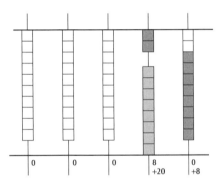

Figure 1.44

Figure 1.45

Doing so, as you can see, is going to "use up" the tens column of beads.

Just as before, we can slide all ten of a "used up" column's beads back up and slide one equivalent bead down from the column to its immediate left (Figure 1.46). In this case, we have, 10 tens = 1 hundred.

Answer: $27 \times 4 = 108$ (Figure 1.47)

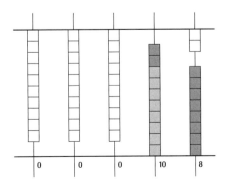

Figure 1.46

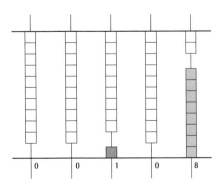

Figure 1.47

4b. Two-digit by two-digit multiplication: 59 × 36 (left to right). (Refer to Figures 1.48–1.54.)

This time, there will just be more arrows to follow in Figure 1.48 below. First, multiply 5 × 3, which is actually 50 × 30 (think 5 × 3 with two zeroes tacked on the end) or 1,500 in Figure 1.49.

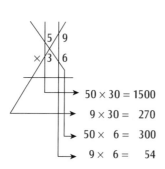

Figure 1.48

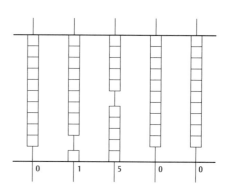

Figure 1.49

Next, multiply 9 × 3, which is actually 9 × 30 (think 9 × 3 with a zero tacked on). Add this number (the product 270) to the 1,500 already on the abacus in Figure 1.50.

In the same way, multiply 5 × 6, which is actually 50 × 6 (think 5 × 6 with a zero tacked on the end). Add this number (the product 300) to the 1,770 already on the abacus (Figure 1.51).

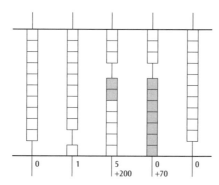

Figure 1.50

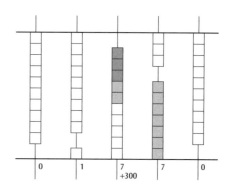

Figure 1.51

What problem do you see?

Since adding 300 will "use up" all the beads in the middle (hundreds) column, slide all ten of them back up and slide down one bead from the column (thousands) to the immediate left (as shown in Figure 1.52).

Finally, multiply 9 × 6 = 54, and add that product to the 2,070 already on the abacus.

What *new* problem do you see?

Although we'd like to add 54, we notice that only three beads are available in the tens column.

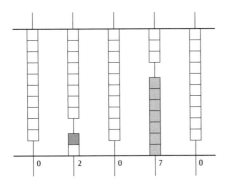

Figure 1.52

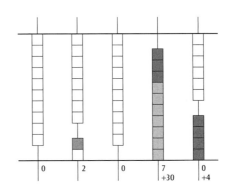

Figure 1.53

An equivalency like the one we performed in the last step won't quite do the trick here. We must slide the remaining three beads down the tens column (Figure 1.53), slide them back up (because we "used up" the column) and slide down a hundred's bead to the immediate left, and then slide two tens beads back down (because $5 - 3 = 2$).

Answer: $59 \times 36 = 2{,}124$ (Figure 1.54)

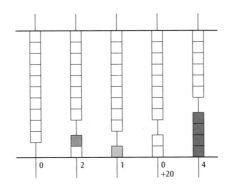

Figure 1.54

Applying the abacus in the classroom is not meant to replace any algorithmic thinking already in use. Nevertheless, it is a wonderful tool for hands-on computation and a real opportunity for students to experience place value and reverse operations (subtraction), and to review multiplication tables and multiplication as multiple addition.

Algebra 2

A high-quality instructional program in Grades K–8 will enable students to:

- Understand patterns, relations, and functions;
- Represent and analyze mathematical situations and structures using algebraic symbols;
- Use mathematical models to represent and understand quantitative relationships; and
- Analyze change in various contexts.

OVERVIEW

The title of the introductory discussion piece, "Catch the Beat," refers to the symbolism of coming to terms with algebra from both an abstract and a pedantic perspective.

Abstractly, algebra is best characterized as "formalized arithmetic," or, as an old professor once explained to our class, "arithmetic with a tuxedo." But what mystifies the confused learner is how in the world arithmetic with its numbers became so complicated when it transformed into algebra with its letters.

Those who tend to "get" algebra don't understand why those who don't get it, don't get it. So, taking another metaphorical approach, the recognition of patterns—an island stopover between the mainlands of arithmetic and algebra—is actually the key to "getting" with algebra.

And even transporting to and from the island of patterns presents an additional challenge. Whereas a trial-and-error solution strategy will eventually lead most students from arithmetic to patterns, it is their working knowledge of thinking strategies (working backwards, solving a simpler problem, etc.) that will move students from patterns more readily to an understanding of algebra.

Pedantically, teachers can get even the youngest of students to embrace patterns (a great help for their later, more formal, study of algebra) through a variety of activities with a sensitivity to their multiple intelligences—colors,

"Growing Patterns" is printed with permission from Nancy Ann Belsky, Presidential Awardee, Mathematics Teacher, 5–8, Westmoreland School, NH.

figures, music, rhymes, poetry, movement games, and so forth. The more often patterns are presented in their myriad of forms, the better for the students.

The rest of the chapter contains four activities: "Growing Patterns" uses colored tiles in three scenarios to literally build numbers and patterns, "Mathemagic" explores the algebraic reasons why certain sequences of operations always end with the same results, "Divide and Conquer" models several fractional relationships with simple paper folding and colored markers, and "Raising the Stakes" generates data and uses line graphs to demonstrate the concept of change.

CATCH THE BEAT

Complete the following pattern: A, A, B, A, A, B, A, A, ___

Most educated adults can hearken back to their high school days and recall with a fair amount of unease the dizzying array of letters and operations known as algebra. They particularly remember having to solve an endless array of equations and to simplify an equal amount of variable expressions—exercises in repetitive and pointless futility for all but the most avid math enthusiast.

However, to see algebra solely through that tainted lens is to miss its true intent. Starting with numbers and challenging us to uncover patterns and to formalize predictive rules (functions), algebra allows us to express complex words and ideas more precisely. It thus becomes a language—much like a romance or a computer language—that transcends the basics (in this case, arithmetic) and opens doors to other worlds (geometry, data analysis, and a whole host of applications).

In short, algebra allows us to communicate mathematically. And, for an elementary teacher, the best part is that the seeds of understanding have already been planted in most students well before they ever set foot in a classroom.

You see, the youngest of children have, at one time or another, been exposed to patterns in disguised forms—nursery rhymes ("E-I-E-I-O"), music on the radio or in church, even poetry ("I do not like Green Eggs and Ham. I do not like them, Sam I Am!"). "When students notice that operations seem to have particular properties, they are beginning to think algebraically" (NCTM, 2000, p. 91).

Returning to the completion problem above, then, the reader would first have to concede that, yes, a pattern exists but that the problem in and of itself is pretty boring. Agreed! But how else could this problem have been presented so that it was more interesting and engaged more students, without compromising its underlying algebraic properties?

How about using colored markers on a dry-erase board or colored transparency pieces on the overhead, or letting students handle colored tiles or colored cubes:

Blue, Blue, Red, Blue, Blue, Red, Blue, Blue, _____?

Or, how about using drawings or pattern blocks:

$\square, \square, \triangle, \square, \square, \triangle, \square, \square, \underline{\hspace{1cm}}?$

Or we could use a keyboard or a toy xylophone to play musical notes, where A = the third shortest bar from the right and B = the second shortest bar from the right:

play the notes:	**xylophone:**
A, A, B, A, A, B, A, A, _____	**C-D-E-F-G-A-B-C**

Or, the students could make lots of cadence noise while everyone sings "We will, we will, rock you!" from Queen's song *We Are the Champions*:)

Stomp! Stomp! Clap! Stomp! Stomp! Clap! Stomp! Stomp! _____

So, how does all of this relate to algebra? As stated previously, we wish to apply some numbers to this exercise and, using the pattern we just identified, try to generalize our findings by creating a function rule (both in words and in algebraic symbols).

Any of the sequences seen so far can have numbers easily applied to them, but let's use the last one here (because it's the most fun to act out!):

Stomp! Stomp! **Clap!** Stomp! Stomp! **Clap!** Stomp! Stomp! _____
   1   2   **3**   4   5   **6**   7   8   **9**

Well, when do we clap? We clap every third beat, which, in mathematical terms, means we clap with the numbers 3, 6, 9, etc. What connects them is that they are all multiples of three, which allows us now to move from just the patterns and to begin using algebraic variables (quantities in alphabet form that change as circumstances warrant):

If T = a trio of "Stomp!, Stomp!, Clap!," and CB = a "Clap!" beat, then $CB = 3 \times T$.

Think about it! For the first trio (T = 1), we would clap at the third beat ($3 \times 1 = 3$); for the second trio (T = 2), we would clap at the sixth beat ($3 \times 2 = 6$); for the third trio (T = 3), we would clap at the ninth beat ($3 \times 3 = 9$), and so on. With this formula, we can now make predictions with confidence, such as:

The twelfth trio will contain the "Clap!" sound at beat 36 (12×3).
The sixtieth beat (a "Clap!") will be at the end of trio 20 ($60 \div 3 = 20$).

And that's not the half of it. The creative intermediate grades teacher could extend this formula into some other student-participation directions, such as students filling in a two-column table with T (Trios) on the left side and CB (the Clap Beat number) on the right side:

T	CB
0	0
1	3
2	6
3	9
4	12
5	15

They would then be given graph paper and asked to plot points (0, 0), (1, 3), (2, 6), etc., from the table just constructed (Trios along the horizontal bottom axis, Clap Beats along the vertical axis).

When the points are connected, the resulting graph is a straight line (linear function)—from which older middle school and high school students could change the T to an "x" and the CB to a "y" to create the new equation y = 3x, leading to a much more abstract conversation around topics like slope. "As students generalize from observations about number and operations, they are forming the basis of algebraic thinking" (NCTM, 2000, p. 93).

That digression notwithstanding, the elementary teacher attuned to standards-based content should consider providing lessons that raise the level of student expectations that NCTM refers to as modeling and patterns, in addition to those already illustrated (patterns and algebraic symbolism)—all of which are targeted items under this Algebra Standard.

Modeling is a powerful tool and can be accomplished fairly quickly through activities such as placing rectangles end to end. Just like before, there will be generated more math than meets the eye but also high levels of student involvement as collected data lead to some new discoveries. "As they study ways to measure geometric objects, students will have opportunities to make generalizations based on patterns" (NCTM, 2000, p. 166).

Rectangular shapes like dominoes work very well to model the following scenario. Have six students sit at a rectangular table (2 along either side, 1 at each end). Now, push a second rectangular table up against the first one so that they are connected end to end, allowing ten students to sit (4 along either side, 1 at each end). With a third table 14 students would be seated, with a fourth table 18 students would be seated, etc.

Here's where the dominoes come in. To help students follow the actual moving of the tables or to help them recall the details of what they just witnessed, dominoes (and a piece of paper and a pencil) serve as models that can help with a drawing or can be placed end to end by the students themselves.

When the data observed and collected is put into the form of a two-column table (T = number of Tables, S = number of Students), it looks like this:

T	S
1	6
2	10
3	14
4	18

The students then proceed as before—look for a pattern, try to come up with a rule (function), and maybe even draw a line on graph paper. (*Answer:* The number of Students turns out to be 4 times the number of Tables, plus 2, or S = [4 × T] + 2.)

GROWING PATTERNS

Guest Contributor: Nancy Ann Belsky

(Grades K–6) (Materials: Colored square tiles, three worksheets, pencil)

NCTM Standard: Students will be able to understand patterns, relations, and functions.

Students of all ages can become excited when exploring pure mathematics. The use of manipulatives allows youngsters to "see" patterns develop as they are physically built. They will interest students of different ability levels, even if those levels are represented in the same classroom.

Square tiles, which are a great manipulative for exploring visual number patterns, are used in the examples that follow. They can be manufactured plastics, ceramic tiles from flooring outlets, or simply cutout cardboard or construction paper squares. Similar activities can be created using differently shaped tiles from pattern block sets.

When using these activities in the classroom, observe what the student is getting out of them and ask questions appropriately. The back-and-forth dialogue created when working through these activities is the most important component of the entire process. Enjoy using these activities to help take all of your students as far as they can "grow"!

Note: Students in Grade K and perhaps even Grade 1 may find the three activities that follow somewhat challenging. The more basic patterns available to these students should be introduced at the discretion of the teacher and may include (but are not limited to):

1. Give 1 tile, add 1. Add a third. Add a fourth . . .
2. Give 1 tile, add 1. Take away 1. Add 2. Take away 2 . . .
3. Give 2 tiles, add 2. Add 2 more. Add 2 more . . .

General Guidelines

Introduce the first activity ("Stair Steps") by modeling the first two steps on the overhead. Make a sample chart on the board (Figure 2.1), and ask a student to come up to the board and record each step as you go along. Let the students hear you think out loud for those first two steps (Figure 2.3 represents a partially completed chart).

Stair Step	# Squares	How I Found It
Ist		
2nd		
3rd		
4th		
5th		

Figure 2.1

Next, ask the class for predictions about the number of tiles needed for the third step. Ask for a student volunteer to come up to the overhead and continue to build it so that you can oversee both that work and the entries on the board (recording of the number of tiles used). If necessary, continue with the fourth step in the same manner.

Now distribute the manipulatives and worksheets (blackline masters can be found in the appendix) for all three activities to the whole class. Ask them to start from the beginning, which you have already demonstrated. All students should be encouraged to keep track of their own work as it progresses. Younger students can paste precut construction paper squares and write the numbers underneath each step in order to record their work. Older students may draw their work on grid paper and then fill in the chart.

As the students work independently or in pairs, circulate throughout the room listening to the students about what is happening with the pattern. After they have built a few stages, ask for a **hypothesis** (educated guess) about the number of tiles in the next step before they build it. They should be able to explain how they came to their various conclusions.

Ask what the number of tiles would be in the next two steps. How did they figure out the totals? Their work should be concluded with a written or oral explanation of how they built the next step in each sequence and their reasoning. Did they find a pattern? If so, have them put it into words.

Older and/or more sophisticated students may be able to tell you in words how they can determine how many blocks must be added for the "nth" Stair Step in the sequence or how many total blocks are used for Stair Step "n." They may also be able to develop a formula or a function that translates those words into mathematics. Be sure students are aware of the order of operations when helping them create those kinds of functions.

All three activities may be presented singly or together. A variation might be to have one activity presented to the whole class and the other two used as workstation or enrichment activities. Students may also be able to create their own patterns to "grow," such as "T-Numbers" as an extension to "Cross Numbers." They might also use other shapes from pattern block sets—triangles, rhombi, or even hexagons—in order to create original patterns to "grow" and share with their classmates.

Activity 1: Stair Step Numbers

These numbers are found by adding the same number of tiles as the (ordinal) Step Number to Figure 2.2. They are also known as **triangular numbers**, in large part because they resemble equilateral triangles as found in ten-pin bowling.

There are at least two methods used to find the total number of tiles at the nth Stair Step.

Method 1: Add all the numbers up to and including the nth number: **1 + 2 + 3 + . . . + n**. (Example: To find the total number of tiles in the 8th Stair Step: $1 + 2 + 3 + 4 + 5 + 6 + 7 + 8 = 36$.)

Method 2: Multiply the number of the Stair Step you want to find the total number of tiles for by the next larger number, then divide your product by 2: **[n × (n + 1)] ÷ 2**. (Example: To find the total number of tiles in the 8th Stair Step: $[8 \times (8 + 1)] \div 2 = [8 \times 9] \div 2 = [72] \div 2 = 36$).

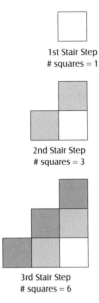

1st Stair Step
squares = 1

2nd Stair Step
squares = 3

3rd Stair Step
squares = 6

Figure 2.2

Stair Step	# Squares	How I Found It
lst	1	1
2nd	3	1 + 2 = 3
3rd	6	1 + 2 + 3 = 6
4th		
5th		

Figure 2.3

Activity 2: Square Squares

A **square number** is found by multiplying any number by itself. This activity will help students make the connection between a square number and its corresponding geometric square. The use of **exponents** may be demonstrated when helping students with the notation. Many students will notice that adding **consecutive odd numbers** to the previous square number creates the next square number ($0 + 1 = 1$, $1 + 3 = 4$, $4 + 5 = 9$, $9 + 7 + 16$, $16 + 9 + 25$, etc.).

There are at least two methods used to find the total number of tiles in the nth Square Square (Figures 2.4 and 2.5).

Method 1: Multiply the number by itself: **n × n**. (Example: To find the total number of tiles in the 8th Square Square: $8 \times 8 = 8^2 = 64$.)

Method 2: Add the number to itself the same number of times it is: **n + n + n + . . . until you have added the number "n" times.** (Example: To find the total number of tiles in the 8th Stair Step: $8 + 8 + 8 + 8 + 8 + 8 + 8 + 8 = 64$.)

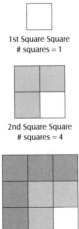

1st Square Square
squares = 1

2nd Square Square
squares = 4

3rd Square Square
squares = 9

Figure 2.4

Square Squares	# Squares	How I Found It
lst	1	1
2nd	4	1 + 3 = 4
3rd	9	1 + 3 + 5 = 9
4th		
5th		

Figure 2.5

Extension to Activity 2. Students who can make the connection between the pattern for the "nth" Square Square (the just seen formula "n × n") and the geometric concept of **area** may find it interesting to extend this activity into finding the **perimeter** of the Square Squares. Be sure to set up for them a systematic method (chart) for keeping track of the data as they generate it.

Questions that may be asked include:

1. Do the numbers get bigger at a faster rate when finding the area or the perimeter? Why or why not?

2. Can you find a "short cut" formula for determining the perimeter of the nth Square Square?

Possible Answers

    a. Four times the length of one side, or, if n = the length of one side, then 4 × n = the perimeter of the nth Square Square (Example: The perimeter of the 8th Square Square = 4 × 8 = 32.)

    b. The length of the side added four times, or n + n + n + n = the perimeter of the nth Square Square (Example: The perimeter of the 8th Square Square = 8 + 8 + 8 + 8 = 32.)

3. Is there a Square Square with the same area and perimeter?
    (Answer: Yes, the 4th Square Square has its area = its perimeter = 16.)

Connecting Activities 1 and 2. For students who have worked on both activities, ask them to compare the two to see if there are any similarities. Perhaps they might see that, in every case, the sum of the number of tiles in two consecutive Stair Steps equals the number of tiles in a Square Square (1 + 3 = 4, 3 + 6 = 9, 6 + 10 = 16, etc.). Students can physically build two consecutive Stair Steps, rotate one of them 180 degrees, and connect the two together to form a Square Square.

Activity 3: Cross Numbers

This activity lends itself to an important transition from concrete building patterns to finding abstract functions that should become easier for students who are encouraged to put their thoughts into words. There are at least three methods used to find the total number of tiles in the nth Cross Number (Figure 2.6 and 2.7).

Method 1: Start with 1 for the first step, then add 4 for every additional step: **1 + 4 + 4 + . . . until you have the number of steps for the nth Cross Number**. (Example: 1 + 4 + 4 + 4 + 4 + 4 + 4 + 4 = 29 tiles for the 8th Cross Number).

Method 2: If n = the Cross Number we want, then start with 1 and then add four times one less than n: **1 + 4 × (n − 1)**. (Example: 1 + 4 × (8 − 1) = 1 + 4 × (7) = 1 + 28 = 29 tiles for the 8th Cross Number.)

Method 3: Multiply the Cross Number we want by 4, then subtract 3 for the 3 tiles we didn't use for the 1st Cross Number: **(4 × n) − 3**. (Example: (4 × 8) − 3 = (32) − 3 = 29 tiles for the 8th Cross Number.)

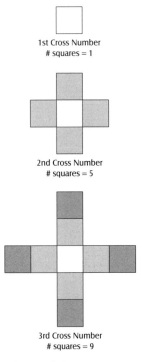

1st Cross Number
squares = 1

2nd Cross Number
squares = 5

3rd Cross Number
squares = 9

Figure 2.6

Cross Number	# Squares	How I Found It
Ist	1	1
2nd	5	1 + 4 = 5
3rd	9	1 + 4 + 4 = 9
4th		
5th		

Figure 2.7

Guest contributor to this section, Nancy Ann Belsky, is a middle school math teacher at Westmoreland School, Westmoreland, NH. Besides her regular teaching duties, including Grades 5–8 and algebra, Nancy Ann is a faculty fellow and site supervisor for student teachers at nearby Keene State College (which, in turn, uses her classroom for middle school mathematics methods classes to observe). Also a collaborator on the joint NASA-NCTM *Mission Mathematics* book and an author of two books of her own, she was the 1991 New Hampshire recipient of the Presidential Award for Excellence in Elementary Mathematics Teaching.

MATHEMAGIC

(Grades 2–8) (Materials: Paper and pencil)

NCTM Standard: Students will be able to represent and analyze mathematical situations and structures using algebraic symbols.

For a nice change of pace, try stimulating your students to a little "mind reading" activity or two. There are a whole bunch of these available in various resource books or that you as the teacher can conjure up yourself.

The real trick, you see, is not only to do these kinds of "Pick-a-Number" games but also to challenge students to figure out why a particular set of instructions always seems to arrive at a predetermined result . . . and to use algebra to prove it to be true!

The steps for two such activities will appear on the left side of the page, their rationale filled in immediately thereafter on the right.

Mathemagic 1

Write down any two-digit number.
Double it.

Add 9 to your product.
Subtract 1 from your sum.
Divide your remainder by 2.
Subtract the original number from your quotient.
The answer will always be 4. Why?

Solution:

Write down any two-digit number:	x
Double it:	2x
Add 9 to your product:	2x + 9
Subtract 1 from your sum:	2x + 9 − 1 = 2x + 8
Divide your remainder by 2:	(2x + 8) ÷ 2 = x + 4
Subtract the original number from your quotient:	x + 4 − x = 4

Alternative Solution:

Write down any two-digit number:	10a + b
Double it:	2(10a + b) = 20a + 2b
Add 9 to your product:	20a + 2b + 9
Subtract 1 from your sum:	20a + 2b + 9 − 1 = 20a + 2b + 8
Divide your remainder by 2:	(20a + 2b + 8) ÷ 2 = 10a + b + 4
Subtract the original number from your quotient:	10a + b + 4 − (10a + b) = 10a + b + 4 − 10a − b = 4

Mathemagic 2

Write down any three-digit number that has all of its digits different.
Form all six possible two-digit permutations that can be made from your original number.
Add all six of those two-digit numbers.
Divide that result by the sum of the digits of your original number.
The answer will always be 22. Why?

Solution:

Write down any three-digit number that has all of its digits different:	100 a + 10b + c
Form all six possible two-digit permutations that can be made from your original number:	10a + b 10b + a 10b + c 10c + b 10a + c 10c + a
Add these six two-digit numbers:	(10a + b) + (10b + a) + (10b + c) + (10c + b) + (10a + c) + (10c + a) = 22a + 22b + 22c
Divide that result by the sum of the digits of your original number:	(22a + 22b + 22c) ÷ (a + b + c) = 22 [a + b + c] ÷ (a + b + c) = 22

DIVIDE AND CONQUER

(Grades 2–8) (Materials: Lots of plain white paper, two colored markers per student)

NCTM Standard: Students will be able to use mathematical models to represent and understand quantitative relationships.

Paper folding is one of the truly fascinating, yet inexpensive, ways to help all students understand the meaning of mathematical ideas. This section will deal with a discovery method for determining reciprocals . . . with a shockingly easy extension into the meaning of the zero exponent.

In the next chapter, we shall examine paper folding with a precut circle to help students uncover a whole bunch of geometric concepts. But in this first part all we need are two sheets of plain white paper for each student.

Part 1

Students should pick up one of their two sheets of paper . . .
Fold it lengthwise (hot dog style) (Figure 2.8) . . .
Crease it right down the middle (Figure 2.9) . . .
And then open it up again (Figure 2.10).
Students should be able to describe what they see before them as "two halves."
Mathematically: $\frac{1}{2} + \frac{1}{2} = 1$ (piece of paper), or $2 \times \frac{1}{2} = 1$
Refold the paper (back to halves). Now, bring the bottom of the half-paper up, and fold it widthwise (hamburger style) (Figure 2.11) . . .

Figure 2.8

Figure 2.9

Figure 2.10

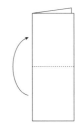

Figure 2.11

Again, crease it in the middle (Figure 2.12) . . .
And then open up the paper again (Figure 2.13).
Students should be able to describe what they see before them as "four fourths."
Mathematically: $\frac{1}{4} + \frac{1}{4} + \frac{1}{4} + \frac{1}{4} = 1$, or $4 \times \frac{1}{4} = 1$
Refold the paper (back to quarters). Now, turn the quarter-paper a quarter turn in either direction, bring one half of the quarter-paper over, and fold it lengthwise (Figure 2.14) . . .
Again, crease it in the middle (Figure 2.15) . . .

Figure 2.12

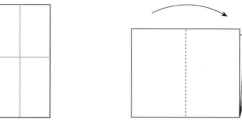

Figure 2.13

Figure 2.14

Figure 2.15

And then open the paper up one more time (Figure 2.16).

Students should be able to describe what they see before them as "eight eighths." Mathematically: $\frac{1}{8} + \frac{1}{8} + \frac{1}{8} + \frac{1}{8} + \frac{1}{8} + \frac{1}{8} + \frac{1}{8} + \frac{1}{8} = 1$, or $8 \times \frac{1}{8} = 1$

Let's summarize what we have so far in chart form (Figure 2.17).

What mathematical relationship exists between the first two columns and then between the last two columns?

Figure 2.16

# Folds	# Pieces	Each Piece Is a . . .
1	2	1/2
2	4	1/4
3	8	1/8

Figure 2.17

In the first case (Columns 1 and 2), the relationship is exponential—in other words, $2^1 = 2$, $2^2 = 4$, and $2^3 = 8$. Each time, the paper is being folded in half again with halves of halves—which makes the base 2. From this pattern, it would appear that the number of pieces $y = 2^x$, where $x =$ the number of folds.

In the second case (Columns 2 and 3), we can formalize the results of folding paper from the previous three pages. Since it appears that the "Each Piece is a . . ." column contains entries that are all 1 divided by corresponding entries in the "# Pieces" column, then the number of pieces y times $(\frac{1}{y})$ always $= 1$ ($2 \times \frac{1}{2}$, $4 \times \frac{1}{4}$, etc.). This concept is known as the **multiplicative inverse**.

Now, ask students to pick up their second sheet of paper. How many folds do they see? None, of course.

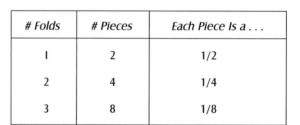

Well, for $y = 2^x$, if, as Figure 2.18 demonstrates, there are no folds ($x = 0$) and there is one piece in the paper ($y = 1$), we may conclude that $1 = 2^0$, which models the elusive concept of the **zero exponent**!

Figure 2.18

Part 2

It could be argued that this part might precede the first—using paper folding in order to gain insight into both the meaning and some simple operations with fractions.

Each student should pick up one of seven additional sheets of paper and fold it "hot dog style" like before (Figure 2.19). Unfold it, take a colored pencil, and color either half of it ($\frac{1}{2}$ = "From 2 equal parts, take 1.") . . .

Now, make two folds like before, and then unfold the paper (Figure 2.20). Students should see a model of this simple proportion:

$$\frac{1}{2} = \frac{2}{4}$$

Now, make three folds like before, and then unfold the paper (Figure 2.21). Students should be able to extend the previous proportion:

$$\frac{1}{2} = \frac{2}{4} = \frac{4}{8}$$

$\frac{1}{2}$

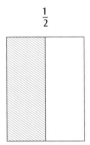

Figure 2.19

$\frac{2}{4}$

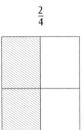

Figure 2.20

$\frac{4}{8}$

Figure 2.21

$\frac{3}{4}$

Figure 2.22

With a new sheet of paper, fold it twice, reopen it, and color three pieces to equal $\frac{3}{4}$ (Figure 2.22).

Now, refold it once more beyond the two folds you just performed, and reopen the paper to see this modeled proportion (Figure 2.23):

$$\frac{3}{4} = \frac{6}{8}$$

Now, with another new sheet of paper, fold it three times, reopen it, and color five pieces to equal $\frac{5}{8}$ (Figure 2.24).

Take another sheet of paper, fold it three times, reopen it, and use a different colored pencil to color three other pieces to equal $\frac{3}{8}$ (Figure 2.25).

Transfer your second color pieces onto the paper with your first color pieces (Figures 2.26 and 2.27):

$\frac{6}{8}$

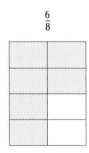

Figure 2.23

$\frac{5}{8}$ + $\frac{3}{8}$ = $\frac{8}{8}$ = 1 (paper)

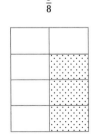

Figure 2.24

+

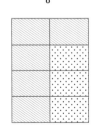

Figure 2.25

=

Figure 2.26

=

Figure 2.27

=

Now, take two new sheets of paper, triple-fold both, and color seven pieces of one (Figure 2.28) and five pieces (different color) of the other (Figure 2.29). We are then going to try to add them:

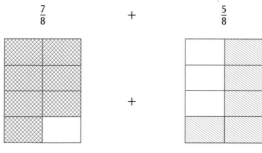

$\frac{7}{8}$ $\qquad$ + $\qquad$ $\frac{5}{8}$

+

Figure 2.28 $\qquad\qquad$ **Figure 2.29**

Transfer one of your second color pieces onto the paper with your first color pieces (remember "give-and-take" from the abacus):

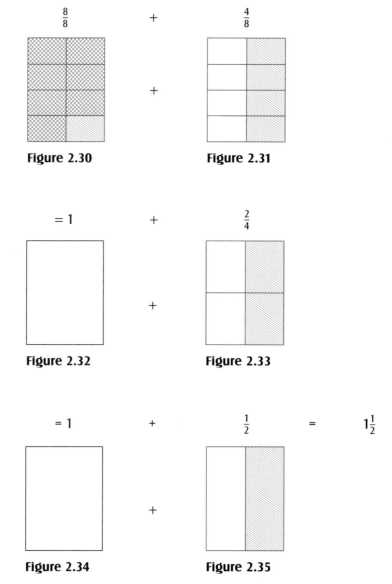

$\frac{8}{8}$ $\qquad$ + $\qquad$ $\frac{4}{8}$

+

Figure 2.30 $\qquad\qquad$ **Figure 2.31**

= 1 $\qquad$ + $\qquad$ $\frac{2}{4}$

+

Figure 2.32 $\qquad\qquad$ **Figure 2.33**

= 1 $\qquad$ + $\qquad$ $\frac{1}{2}$ $\qquad$ = $\qquad$ $1\frac{1}{2}$

+

Figure 2.34 $\qquad\qquad$ **Figure 2.35**

And, if needed, the mixed number can then be converted into a decimal (1.5) or into an improper fraction ($\frac{3}{2}$).

RAISING THE STAKES

(Grades 5–8) (Materials: Lots of 1st-quadrant graph paper, ruler, pencil)

NCTM Standard: Students will be able to analyze change in various contexts.

This unit takes a real-world situation involving a brother and a sister and studies what happens mathematically when decisions are made that affect changes in their business relationship. There will be an emphasis here on the use of heuristics (thinking strategies), such as making charts and drawing graphs, as well as supporting those decisions with algebraic reasoning.

Here's some background information:

> Jim and Lucy are brother and sister. Both are teenagers, although Jim is old enough to drive a car while Lucy is not.
>
> They live about a mile away from a neighborhood with two families with small children. The parents of these children need either Jim or Lucy to babysit every Saturday night.

Scenario 1: Both Jim and Lucy take babysitting jobs on the same Saturday night. Both jobs pay $3 per hour, but Jim negotiates an extra $4 up front for gas money.

As is illustrated in Figure 2.36, although Jim and Lucy are essentially performing the same service, the $4 gap between their earnings is constant:

Hours X	Jim 3x + 4	Lucy 3x
0	3(0) + 4 = 4	3(0) = 0
1	3(1) + 4 = 7	3(1) = 3
2	3(2) + 4 = 10	3(2) = 6
3	3(3) + 4 = 13	3(3) = 9
4	3(4) + 4 = 16	3(4) = 12

Figure 2.36

That disparity is highlighted in the last column of Figure 2.37 (3x + 4 − 3x = 4) and in the graph of the constant function (horizontal line) in Figure 2.38.

Hours X	Jim 3x + 4	Lucy 3x	Difference (3x + 4) − 3x = 4
0	4	0	(4) − 0 = 4
1	7	3	(7) − 0 = 4
2	10	6	(10) − 6 = 4
3	13	9	(13) − 9 = 4
4	16	12	(16) − 12 = 4

Figure 2.37

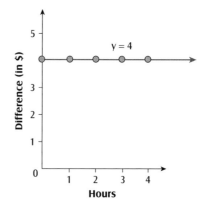

Figure 2.38

Scenario 2: Lucy finds out about this inequity and, since she doesn't yet drive a car, she negotiates a better deal for herself the following Saturday night.

She would now receive $5 per hour for her babysitting services, while Jim would still receive $3 per hour and $4 upfront for gas for his car as shown in Figure 2.39.

Note that, while Jim starts out making more money, eventually Lucy catches up to the point where they are making the same:

$$5x = 3x + 4$$
$$\underline{-3x \quad -3x}$$
$$2x = 0 + 4$$
$$2x = 4$$
$$x = 2 \text{ hours}$$

Note how the graph in Figure 2.40 below also reflects the fact that, at the 2-hour point, Jim and Lucy are making the same amount of money ($10). Beyond that, Lucy makes more than Jim (inequality):

$$5x > 3x + 4$$
$$\underline{-3x \quad -3x}$$
$$2x > 4$$
$$x > 2 \text{ hours}$$

Hours X	Jim 3x + 4	Lucy 5x
0	3(0) + 4 = 4	5(0) = 0
1	3(1) + 4 = 7	5(1) = 5
2	3(2) + 4 = 10	5(2) = 10
3	3(3) + 4 = 13	5(3) = 15
4	3(4) + 4 = 16	5(4) = 20

Figure 2.39

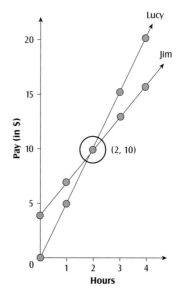

Figure 2.40

In fact, if one studies the graph, Lucy's wage is indeed "above" Jim's after the 2-hour point. By the same token, Lucy's wage is "below" Jim's for the time *before* that (x < 2).

Extensions: There are some other ways to analyze Lucy's "new deal":

1. Examine the different characteristics—the slope and y-intercept—of the lines in Figure 2.40 (y = mx + b).

2. Compare the learning impact of the composite function graph (Figure 2.41) against that of the chart (Figure 2.42).

(The chart tells a much clearer story—especially as it pertains to 3x + 4 − 5x = 4 − 2x, the algebraic expression for the difference between Jim's and Lucy's current deals.)

The gap between Jim and Lucy's income diminishes by the hour (an **arithmetic progression**, if you will). Note how the numbers turn negative after Hour 2, indicating that Lucy's new deal creates a higher income than Jim's the longer she babysits.

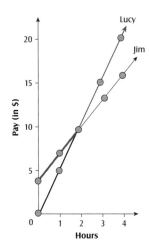

Figure 2.41

Hours X	Jim 3x + 4	Lucy 5x	Difference (3x + 4) − 5x = 4 − 2x
0	4	0	(4) − 0 = 4 − 2(0) = 4
1	7	5	(7) − 5 = 4 − 2(1) = 2
2	10	10	(10) − 10 = 4 − 2(2) = 0
3	13	15	(13) − 15 = 4 − 2(3) = −2
4	16	20	(16) − 20 = 4 − 2(4) = −4

Figure 2.42

Scenario 3: After thinking about this situation for a while, Jim, being the elder, decides it's time to "pull rank" on his sister. His idea for next Saturday night is that, at the end of two hours, he and Lucy would switch babysitting assignments so that he can ensure himself the larger payout.

Following the algebra provides the clues for understanding this scenario. If Jim wants to create a rule (or function) for his "new deal," he needs to subtract: 3x + 4 − 5x = 4 − 2x. That being said, he is also not going to accept a negative difference (as it compares with Lucy)—which is why we have to take the **absolute value** of 4 − 2x (which will ensure a positive result as seen in Figure 2.43).

The graph below confirms that reasoning. The ray represents the negative difference Jim experienced after 2 hours of work from the point (2, 0) under the x-axis (Figure 2.44).

What the absolute value does is take that ray and reflect it above (flip over) the x-axis, creating the classic "V-shaped" graph. In that way, there is never a negative difference (all the $ values are either 0 or positive).

Note: However, Scenario 3 was never really put into practice. In the time Jim and Lucy would be switching houses, the children for whom they are caring would have been left unattended.

Hours X	Jim 3x + 4	Lucy 5x	Absolute Value of Difference | 4 − 2x |
0	4	0	| 4 − 2(0) | = | 4 | = 4
1	7	5	| 4 − 2(1) | = | 2 | = 2
2	10	10	| 4 − 2(2) | = | 0 | = 0
3	13	15	| 4 − 2(3) | = | −2 | = 2
4	16	20	| 4 − 2(4) | = | −4 | = 4

Figure 2.43

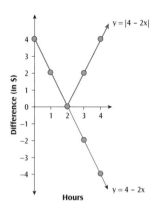

Figure 2.44

Scenario 4: Jim and Lucy finally decided to reach a compromise for the following Saturday night. They will pool whatever money they receive, and split that amount in half (find the **average** per Figure 2.45).

It is important to remember that, whenever one divides a polynomial like 8x + 4 by a monomial like 2, both the 8x and the 4 get divided by the 2:

The general form of the average function, denoted by (Y1 + Y2) ÷ 2, varies little in process from the one determining the value of a statistical average such as mean. As we can see in Figure 2.46, its visual representation is that of an angle bisector and can be verified as such by utilizing geometric tools such as a protractor or even a compass and straightedge.

(Incidentally, Scenario 5 would have Mom and yours truly as Dad taking charge of Jim and Lucy's money or "strongly encouraging" them to get out of the babysitting business altogether if a compromise could not be reached!)

Hours X	Jim 3x + 4	Lucy 5x	Average [8x + 4] ÷ 2 = 4x + 2
0	4	0	[8(0) + 4] ÷ 2 = 4(0) + 2 = 2
1	7	5	[8(1) + 4] ÷ 2 = 4(1) + 2 = 6
2	10	10	[8(2) + 4] ÷ 2 = 4(2) + 2 = 10
3	13	15	[8(3) + 4] ÷ 2 = 4(3) + 2 = 14
4	16	20	[8(4) + 4] ÷ 2 = 4(4) + 2 = 18

Figure 2.45

Figure 2.46

In retrospect, it's interesting from a mathematical perspective to see how one change can have such a profound effect on the algebra, not to mention the numbers and the geometry. Graphs develop points of equilibrium, sharp corners, or ricochets off an axis—all because one person in a two-party arrangement wished to change the rules slightly.

And, just like in real life, it's certainly true, yet mysterious, that the one true constant is change. How we cope with that paradox (e.g., encouraging our students to use heuristics more often) goes a long way toward our success in the studying and teaching of mathematics.

Geometry 3

A high-quality instructional program in Grades K–8 will enable students to:

- Analyze characteristics and properties of two- and three-dimensional geometric shapes and develop some mathematical arguments about geometric relationships;

- Specify locations and describe spatial relationships using coordinate geometry and other representations;

- Apply transformations and use symmetry to analyze mathematical situations; and

- Use visualization, spatial reasoning, and geometric modeling to solve problems.

OVERVIEW

Take any book and stand it on its bottom end with the cover facing you. Next, loosely "pinch" the upper right corner of the book—that is, your right thumb should be at the top right front cover and your right index finger should be around on the top left back cover.

Now, with your left hand, gradually open the book and notice what happens to the distance between your right thumb and index finger. The wider the angle (the opening between the front and back covers), the further apart your right thumb and index finger become.

And, so it is with any triangle—the largest angle (if one is greater than the other two) is always across from the longest (opposite) side.

This is one way in which triangles "happen." In fact, all geometric figures happen; that is, they have ongoing interrelationships that form the basis for so much of our formal mathematics. The key to learning about these relationships is literally to play around with the figures themselves—make them, measure them, flip them, turn them, and expand them.

"Hands-On Shapes" is printed with permission from Denise Edelson, Master Teacher, Chicago Public Schools, IL.

In fact, in much the same way that master sculptors mold wet clay or a fine chef gives and takes ingredients to prepare a sumptuous meal, an expert teacher encourages students to get really involved with the material—and, for success in math, specifically geometry, this is especially true.

After the "Make Figures 'Happen'" discussion piece, the rest of the chapter lists the following activities: "Hands-On Shapes" has a set of seven ways to use various manipulatives with early elementary grade students, "Guess My Pattern" features creativity with the identification of four-color grid patterns, "Crazy Quilts" offers a different take on building five-cube letters and placing them on a checkerboard, and "Fold It Right There!" takes a cut-out paper circle and a ruler and opens the door to no fewer than thirty-five mathematical concepts.

MAKE FIGURES "HAPPEN"

Besides simplicity, what we are looking for in our lesson planning is energy—putting ideas into motion—so that, much like cell mitosis, student thinking can be encouraged to expand and connections can be encouraged to evolve.

Along with plain white (reamed) paper, give students access to safety scissors, markers, and a metric ruler prior to embarking on a flexible exploration activity in geometry that can be tailored to match their abilities. It is your call as teacher to decide to what extent your assistance is needed at various stages of this exercise.

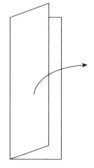

Figure 3.1

1. Take a piece of paper, and, with the shorter side along the bottom, fold the paper "hot dog style" (or lengthwise) with a vertical crease right down the middle (Figure 3.1). Then, open the paper back up.

The next step necessitates some instructional judgment on your part. There are several options open to you here, but they are all fundamentally directed toward making an equilateral triangle with its upper vertex located along that middle crease.

Your knowledge of your students' capabilities will go a long way in determining how best to proceed.

Figure 3.2

2. Basically, use the bottom (the shorter length) of the paper as the measure for each of the three sides of the equilateral triangle.

To do this, pull the bottom left corner of the paper up along the middle crease and keep sliding that corner up until you make a perfect point in the bottom right corner (Figure 3.2). When that happens, you have found the upper vertex of the equilateral triangle you're in the midst of creating.

Use a marker to mark the vertex—but, if at all possible, do ***not*** fold the paper.

Note: Some teachers prefer that their students, after opening their papers back to the original form (without a second crease, as suggested), use their markers and rulers to draw the remaining two sides of the equilateral triangle (vertex to bottom left corner, vertex to bottom right corner).

Other teachers have their students ignore the author's suggestion, make that second crease, and then use that crease with their markers to draw one side of the equilateral triangle (vertex to bottom right corner). It's a good idea for the short run, but that move will create too many creases for later on in the activity.

3. Repeat the process accompanying the figure above, only now **pull** the right corner up along the middle crease and keep sliding it up until you make a perfect point in the bottom left corner (Figure 3.3).

Figure 3.3

4. If you used a marker and have been tracing at any point during steps 2 and 3, your unraveled paper will now contain the outline of an equilateral triangle (Figure 3.4 with the middle crease not drawn for emphasis).

Otherwise, the only thing that should appear on your paper at this point (besides the middle crease) is the vertex.

5. If you have been tracing, use your ruler and marker very carefully to extend the two already drawn sides of the equilateral triangle so that they reach the top of the paper (Figure 3.5).

However, if you only have a marked vertex on your paper, simply make two slanted creases—one through the vertex and the bottom left corner of the paper (making a perfect point), the other through the vertex and the bottom right corner of the paper (another perfect point).

Figure 3.4

6. Finally, number your paper as indicated in Figure 3.6 below.

Question: How many triangles are there on your paper?

Answer: Six. (The two equilateral triangles—one large and one small—are, in turn, each comprised of two right triangles [numbered 1 to 4].)

Figure 3.5

More Classroom Suggestions

Grades K–2

Younger children need practice with measurement (Chapter 4) and whole-number operations (Chapter 1). To that end, you might want to consider altering the dimensions of the paper your students will be using.

An 8.5 in.-by-11 in. piece of plain white paper equals 21.6 cm-by-27.8 cm in metric measure. Measure and trim widths and lengths to 20 cm-by-26 cm.

Figure 3.6

1. Note how the slanted lines/creases in Figure 3.6 intersect the top and bottom widths of the paper. Since the middle crease makes halfway points top and bottom, the bases of right triangles 1 and 2 should equal 10 cm apiece and the bases of right triangles 3 and 4 should equal 5 cm apiece. And, if students want to cut out right triangles 3 and 4, the two remaining segments of the top width of the original paper should also equal 5 cm apiece:

$$5 + 5 = 10, \ 10 - 5 = 5, \ 10 + 5 = 15, \ 15 - 5 = 10, \ 15 - 10 = 5$$
$$10 + 10 = 20, \ 5 + 5 + 5 + 5 = 20, \ 10 + 10 = 5 + 5 + 5 + 5$$
$$20 - 5 = 15, \ 20 - 10 = 10, \ 20 - 15 = 5$$
$$2 \times 5 = 10, \ 2 \times 10 = 20, \ 4 \times 5 = 20$$
$$2 \times 10 = 4 \times 5, \ 20 \div 2 = 10, \ 20 \div 4 = 5$$

2. Put triangles 1 and 2 and triangles 3 and 4 back together (if detached) in order to create the large and small equilateral triangles. As the word implies, "**equilateral**" means equal-sided, with each side of the small equilateral triangle 10 cm and each side of the large equilateral triangle 20 cm.

Introduce another term, perimeter (adding all the sides), to encourage not only more operational thinking but also some comparative thinking with fractions:

$$10 + 10 + 10 = 3 \times 10 = 30, \; 30 \div 3 = 10$$
$$(10 + 10) + 10 = 20 + 10 = 30, \; 30 - 10 = 20, \; 30 - 20 = 10$$
$$20 + 20 + 20 = 60, \; 3 \times 20 = 60, \; 60 \div 3 = 20$$
$$(20 + 20) + 20 = 40 + 20 = 60, \; 60 - 20 = 40, \; 60 - 40 = 20$$
$$\frac{10}{20} = \frac{1}{2}, \frac{20}{40} = \frac{2}{4} = \frac{1}{2}, \frac{30}{60} = \frac{3}{6} = \frac{1}{2},$$
$$\frac{10}{30} = \frac{1}{3}, \frac{20}{60} = \frac{2}{6} = \frac{1}{3}$$

3. Without having to introduce a formal definition of "area," give students access to several copies of the small equilateral triangle (right triangles 3 and 4 together).

Question: How many small equilateral triangles can fit within the boundaries of the large equilateral triangle (right triangles 1 and 2 together)?

Answer: Four. (For every one large equilateral triangle, there are four small equilateral triangles inside—a "ratio" of 1 to 4, or $\frac{1}{4}$.)

Question: How many small right triangles (either the numbered 3 or 4) can fit within the boundaries of the large equilateral triangle?

Answer: Eight. (For every one large equilateral triangle, there are eight small right triangles inside—a ratio of 1 to 8, or $\frac{1}{8}$.)

Figure 3.7

4. Now give your students access to several copies of the large equilateral triangle cut into separate right triangles 1 and 2 and a copy of the predrawn "net" paper as shown in Figure 3.7. (See the appendix for a blackline master.)

With a transparency of the net on the overhead, you can demonstrate how to use two of the right triangles to introduce/construct some other geometric figures (clockwise from the upper right corner in Figure 3.8)—rectangle, **parallelogram** (one with a shorter diagonal, a second with a longer one), and a **right trapezoid** (using three cutout right triangles to build).

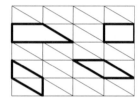

Figure 3.8

5. Students should quickly discover that, given any one of the geometric figures just illustrated, it can be moved (like chess or checker pieces) anywhere around the net—the concept of "slide" (or, more formally, **translation**).

Students should also be challenged to construct, as one example, a bigger rectangle. By making, say, a rectangle four times the size of its original (using eight right triangles to do so) they should begin to notice "growth" or "expanding" (or, more formally, **dilation**).

6. For some creative discovery, let students do one or both of two things. One would be to let them use different-colored markers with net paper to create some interesting visual geometric patterns on their own.

The other would be to break out some pattern blocks to do something similar on their desks but of a more hands-on nature. The different combinations of shapes and colors can produce some truly interesting and unique student art.

Grades 3–5

(Alterations to the K–2 suggestions just mentioned.)

1. Trimming regularly dimensioned 21.6 cm-by-27.8 cm paper to the proposed 20 cm-by-26 cm is optional if you would prefer that your students work with some fractions and their operations (rather than whole numbers).

With the slanted line intersections at the top and bottom of the paper and the middle crease in place, label the bases of right triangles 1 and 2 $= \frac{1}{2}$ apiece and the bases of right triangles 3 and 4 $= \frac{1}{4}$ apiece. In addition, the two segments of the top width of the original paper outside of the slanted lines can also be labeled $= \frac{1}{4}$ apiece:

$$\frac{1}{2} + \frac{1}{2} = \frac{2}{2} = 1, \; 2 \times (\frac{1}{2}) = \frac{2}{2} = 1, \; 1 \div 2 = \frac{1}{2}, \; 1 \div 4 = \frac{1}{4}$$

$$\frac{1}{4} + \frac{1}{4} = \frac{2}{4} = \frac{1}{2}, \; 2 \times (\frac{1}{4}) = \frac{2}{4} = \frac{1}{2}$$

$$\frac{1}{4} + \frac{1}{2} = \frac{1}{4} + (\frac{1}{4} + \frac{1}{4}) = 3 \times (\frac{1}{4}) = \frac{3}{4}, \; \frac{3}{4} + \frac{1}{4} = \frac{4}{4} = 1$$

$$\frac{1}{2} - \frac{1}{4} = \frac{2}{4} - \frac{1}{4} = \frac{1}{4}, \; \frac{3}{4} - \frac{1}{4} = \frac{2}{4} = \frac{1}{2}, \; 1 - \frac{1}{4} = \frac{4}{4} - \frac{1}{4} = \frac{3}{4}$$

2 and 3. Cut out the small and large equilateral triangles. The concept of comparison, or **ratio**, should be self-evident from the labels on the bases of the two triangles—the smaller triangle's base equals $\frac{1}{4} + \frac{1}{4} = \frac{1}{2}$, and the larger triangle's base equals $\frac{1}{2} + \frac{1}{2} = 1$. Since the same comparison works for all three sides of both triangles respectively, we can conclude that the ratio of the lengths of the sides of the small equilateral triangle to the large one equals $\frac{1}{2}$.

In addition and as done previously, since four small equilateral triangles can be traced inside the large one, we can also conclude that the ratio of the areas of the small equilateral triangle to the large one equals $\frac{1}{4}$.

4. Having already seen how figures can "slide" (translate) on a net, students should be ready to handle "turn" (**rotation**) and "flip" (**reflection**).

Place your two cutout equilateral triangles vertex to vertex (as seen in Figure 3.6 before they were cut out). Using the vertex as a "pivot point" (point of rotation), rotate the upper (small) equilateral triangle a half-turn (or 180°) until it fits inside of the large equilateral triangle.

We have already determined that the sides of the small and large equilateral triangles are in a 1:2 ratio (thus, in **proportion**). And, using a protractor, we can also measure the paired-off (**corresponding**) angles of the respective triangles and see a match for each pair (60°). Thus, it is said that the two triangles are **similar** to each other (one is the dilation of the other).

5. For either of the cutout equilateral triangles, the middle crease (known more formally as a **perpendicular bisector**) allows one of the right triangles on one half to fold perfectly atop its counterpart on the other side. This visual one-to-one relationship is called **congruency** and plays a major role in geometry courses taught in high school.

Even though one half of either equilateral triangle is the reverse image of the other, we still say that the equilateral triangle has **symmetry**. For a vertical crease (as is the case here), our triangles are said to have **vertical-line symmetry**; under different circumstances and for a horizontal crease, any other figure would have **horizontal-line symmetry**.

6. A nice follow-up activity for students is to explore the various symmetries of the English (block) alphabet. For example, the letter **A** has vertical-line symmetry (an imaginary vertical line right down the middle would cut the letter into two congruent halves), and the letter **B** has horizontal-line symmetry.

There are some letters—**X** comes to mind—that demonstrate both types of line symmetry. And there are some, such as the letter **H**, which demonstrate **rotational**, or **point, symmetry** (a half-turn around an imaginary center point reveals the same letter) in addition to both types of line symmetry.

After your class examines all 26 block letters for the three aforementioned symmetries, have them determine a "Symm-Score" for each of their names. For example, my full first name—**TIMOTHY**—would be worth 13 points. (Can you, as the reader, determine that score yourself?)

Another question: How many letters have all three symmetries (and are worth 3 Symm-Score points apiece)?

Answer: Four (**H, I, O,** and **X**).

Grades 6–8

(No particular order or connection to previous steps)

1.   An **isometry** is a distance-preserving transformation (a translation, rotation, and reflection are; a dilation is not).

What eventually happens in the middle grades is that, whether they are aware of it or not, students become challenged by the visual combinations of the above distance-preserving transformations. One difficulty involves the notion of **orientation** of the original figure: How does reading the order of the vertices of the original figure in either a clockwise or counter-clockwise direction change that order in the final image of the original after transformation(s)?

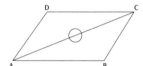

Figure 3.9

Neither a translation nor a rotation will alter orientation, making both transformations direct isometries. However, a single reflection will, making that transformation an indirect (or opposite) isometry.

Figures 3.9 and 3.10 give a little more insight as to how students can study properties of geometric figures . . . but also why others might not see so clearly.

In parallelogram ABCD (Figure 3.9), a center of rotation is drawn on the diagonal so that lower triangle CBA might be rotated a half-turn and rest upon (be congruent to, have a one-to-one correspondence with) upper triangle ADC. Even though a direct isometry, notice how point C corresponds with point A and point A corresponds with point C—a possible cause of confusion for many students.

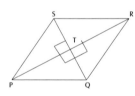

Figure 3.10

In equilateral parallelogram PQRS (Figure 3.10) (better known as a **rhombus**), both diagonals are drawn. They bisect each other (as they do in any parallelogram), but they are also perpendicular to each other—thus creating four right triangles. Rotating half-turns around point T, opposite right triangles preserve orientation with each other but adjacent ones do not (as they are reflections of each other over the half-diagonal they share).

2.   Recognizing the combination of two lines of reflection is a step in the right direction because there are only two possible cases, both of which having fairly routine processes attached.

First, demonstrate (perhaps with graph paper) how any line of reflection (or "mirror line") acts as a perpendicular bisector for the invisible segments joining all points of the original figure (**pre-image**) with their result (**image**).

In Figure 3.11, the original triangle (pre-image) ABC is reflected over mirror line m to create reflected (image) triangle A´B´C´. (The accent marks indicate that some kind of transformation has taken place).

Case 1: When the two mirror lines (in Figure 3.12, m and n) are parallel to each other, the image of the image (double-reflected triangle A"B"C") is just a translation of the pre-image.

Case 2: When the two mirror lines intersect, the image of the image (A"B"C") is a rotation of the pre-image around the point of intersection of those two mirror lines as shown in Figure 3.13.

The number of degrees of rotation equals twice the measure of the angle between the mirror lines. (Since the mirror lines in the figure at the right are perpendicular, the degrees of rotation equal $2 \times 90° = 180°$ = half-turn.)

3. Reversing the process of giving younger students net paper and having them color in various triangular regions, encourage the older ones to take various geometric figures of their own choosing and completely tile (without gaps or overlaps) a piece of graph paper or a plain white piece of paper. Pattern blocks may help more hands-on learners get a better feel for this task.

Successful students will not only create visual patterns with repeating squares, hexagons, etc., but will also demonstrate their knowledge of transformations in making what is known as a **tessellation**. For some ideas that will make an immediate and lasting impression on most, such an activity might be preceded by an Internet search of the great tessellation artist, M.C. Escher.

A real-world activity that may also be of interest to your students would be to encourage them to travel about their locality and take digital photos (if accessible) of examples of tessellations in nearby buildings and landmarks. There are also numerous examples of symmetry that can be found in nature (e.g., the human body), as well as transformations within musical compositions and choreographed dance routines (or even ballroom or square dancing).

4. Figure 3.14 below resembles "footprints in the sand" made by some two-legged mechanical creature with triangular feet walking north (in the direction of the middle axis). In reality, though, this combination of transformations is known as a **glide reflection**.

Question: What transformations are present here?

Answer: Starting with the right triangle in the lower left corner, one may think of a glide reflection as a series of translation-reflections or reflection-translations.

HANDS-ON SHAPES

Guest Contributor: Denise Edelson

(Grades K–2) (Materials: Listed by each activity below)

NCTM Standard: Students will be able to analyze characteristics and properties of two- and three-dimensional geometric shapes and develop mathematical arguments about geometric relationships.

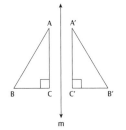

Figure 3.11

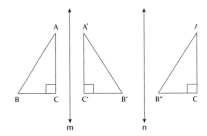

Figure 3.12

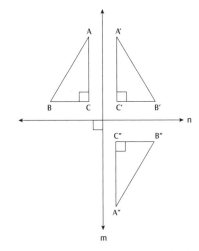

Figure 3.13

Figure 3.14

Among the many aspects to which the beginning teacher is forced to adhere is writing a lesson plan consistent with standards practice and distinguishing between the goal of the lesson (thinking processes) and the activity itself.

The following four activities address the NCTM benchmark stated above and are each arranged in a clear and concise lesson plan format. There is also a paragraph devoted to differentiated instruction (Teacher Expectations and Adaptations) for teachers to consider for a wider range of student abilities.

Activity 1 (Grades PreK–K)

Goal: Students will sort beads to identify and distinguish between two-dimensional shapes.

Activity: Students sort beads by shape. The teacher encourages the oral use of mathematical vocabulary (square, triangle, etc.). Students will then draw an example of each shape in their individual math journals.

Materials: Sorting trays (or compartmentalized paper plates), beads of various shapes, individual math journals, drawing/writing tools

Evaluation: Observe students as they sort the beads. Discuss the activity with individual students to encourage the use of and greater ease with math vocabulary. Lead a class discussion, noting the comments from individual students as they discuss the occurrence of these shapes in their everyday lives.

Teacher Expectations and Adaptations: More advanced students may be asked to sort by more than one characteristic—perhaps by shape and size—or to sort a combination of two- and three-dimensional shapes. They might also make statements about the shapes that the teacher may copy in their journals. Students may also cut out pictures from magazines of objects that match these shapes (soup cans, balls, etc.) and glue them into their math journals. Less advanced students may not be able to draw shapes but might trace shapes drawn by the teacher.

Activity 2 (Grades 1–2)

Goal: Students will become familiar with two-dimensional geometric shapes and their geometric relationships through tactile positioning of these shapes, using math manipulatives.

Activity: Using pattern blocks, students will make designs identical to a partner's design while working side by side in pairs.

Materials: Pattern blocks, student work area that allows the side-by-side positioning of pairs of students

Evaluation: Teacher observation of completed designs and of student oral interaction during their construction

Teacher Expectations and Adaptations: Students will be encouraged to use geometric vocabulary while constructing and discussing designs. To ensure equal participation, student pairs may be instructed to take turns placing shapes to be added to their designs. The total number of pattern blocks may be predetermined by the teacher to accommodate time restrictions or the ability levels of the students. If there is time, students may disassemble their constructions together, one piece (or one shape) at a time, so as to reinforce the identification of specific shapes and their position in the construction.

Activity 3 (Grades 1–2)

Goal: Students construct two-dimensional designs and then transfer a different physical representation of the same idea.

Activity: Students will build two-dimensional designs with pattern blocks and then reproduce them in their math journals, using paper precut to the size and shape of the pattern blocks. Students should use geometric terms (the names of their shapes) while writing to comment on this experience, including commenting on any construction problems or interesting patterns they encountered.

Materials: Individual math journals, drawing/writing utensils, pattern blocks, paper precut to the size and shape of the pattern blocks

Evaluation: Teacher and student compare paper reproduction to the original pattern block design, noting differences (if any). Ask each student questions about the construction, encouraging the use of mathematical vocabulary. Conduct a class discussion, asking for comments on characteristics or properties of the geometric shapes manipulated in this activity.

Teacher Expectations and Adaptations: Elements of symmetry will be reinforced by teacher comments, as will one-to-one correspondence of individual pattern pieces. The number of pieces may be limited for younger or less advanced students. More advanced students might be asked to construct more complicated designs.

Activity 4 (Grades 1–2)

Goal: Students construct three-dimensional designs and then transfer a different physical representation of the same idea.

Activity: Working as partners, students build a three-dimensional design using full-size Hex-a-Link Cubes and then reproduce this construction using similarly shaped but smaller Centicubes. Students describe this activity in their individual math journals, which may be read aloud. The rest of the class will be encouraged to ask questions or comment on the interesting designs made by their classmates.

Materials: Hex-a-Link Cubes, Centicubes, individual student math journals, drawing/writing utensils

Evaluation: The teacher observes student constructions, evaluates written analyses in individual math journals, and evaluates oral presentations and answers to questions posed by classmates.

Teacher Expectations and Adaptations: These constructions may be displayed at the math center in the classroom. A comment sheet may be made available next to each pair of constructions (one a full-sized model, the other a smaller model) for comments from students. Students will observe and compare the similarities and differences in each pair of constructions. When two students work together, there should be a continual monitoring of spatial placement and patterning/matching. Less advanced students may be limited in the number of cubes that they use. More advanced students might be asked to match color placement as well as spatial placement of their cubes.

Alternative Activities (Grades PreK–2)

1. Place a plastic grid mat (or a portion of a shower curtain with drawn grid lines) on the classroom floor, place two- and/or three-dimensional shapes on the mat, and ask students to identify shapes that are "near to, under, or above" other shapes.

Differentiations: Allow students who are more able to make up their own questions that other students may answer. If the students are able, they may label the "x" and "y" axes (with numbers or with numbers and letters) and name the location of shapes using coordinate points. This activity may also be done using the overhead projector with an acetate grid mat and transparent colored two- and three-dimensional shapes (alternative games: Twister, Battleship).

2. In their math journals, students trace and label pictures of triangles, squares, and other two-dimensional shapes that have been precut by the teacher out of cardboard or heavy paper. Students then trace each shape in a variety of different attitudes—turning it, sliding it, and/or flipping it—and must do so at least four times.

Differentiations: More advanced students may make a design as they trace the shapes. If less advanced students have difficulty identifying in writing the names of those two-dimensional shapes or are unable to label their shapes, the teacher may ask those students to identify the cardboard cutouts in words, making sure to ask each child to do so from at least two different attitudes.

3. Students identify and cut out pictures in magazines that match two- and three-dimensional shapes (soup cans, balls, etc.) and glue them into their individual math journals.

Differentiations: Students who can write may label the pictures that they find or make a list of objects in the classroom or in their environment that match the shapes they are studying.

Guest contributor to this section, Denise Edelson, is an elementary teacher at Hannah G. Solomon Elementary School in Chicago, Illinois. She was the 1999 Illinois recipient of the Presidential Award for Excellence in Elementary Mathematics Teaching. She obtained a Master of Science degree in education from Northern Illinois University in 2000 and then went on to achieve National Board Certification as a Middle Childhood Generalist in 2002. She has also authored articles on mathematics teaching that have appeared in National Council of Teachers of Mathematics publications, *Empowering the Beginning Teacher of Mathematics: Elementary School* and *Empowering the Beginning Teacher of Mathematics: Middle School*, published in 2004.

GUESS MY PATTERN

(Grades K–4) (Materials: Lots of worksheets, four same-colored markers or pencils per student)

NCTM Standard: Students will be able to specify locations and describe spatial relationships using coordinate geometry and other representational systems.

Here's a nice activity that enables students to create their own colorful matrix patterns and to try to visualize and reconstruct those created by others.

The materials required for each student consist of sixteen interlocking cubes (four from each of four colors: black, blue, green, and red), four same-colored pencils, and a double-sided "playing board" (a piece of grid paper) as shown in Figure 3.15. (See appendix for a blackline master.)

The in-class process itself is fun and totally engaging. The steps:

1. The teacher must first prepare several grid transparencies (for use on the overhead projector). Using four overhead pens (black, blue, green, and red), he or she takes a grid and colors four boxes with one color, four with another, and so forth, so that each color follows a clear, visible pattern (such as in Figure 3.16).

The patterns can be pretty unimaginative (as in the previous matrix) or something a little more interesting (Figure 3.17). The point here is that the teacher needs to prepare some visual examples—over a predetermined range of complexity—for classroom use on the overhead.

2. The teacher then organizes each student's materials and handouts in preparation for class.

3. Class begins with a couple of overhead examples being displayed. (The teacher should keep one or two of them out of sight for now.) Students then remove the sixteen cubes from each of their bags (no pencils yet) and, using one side of grid paper, make their own individual colored matrices.

4. The teacher traverses the room, offering help when needed but also judging the quality of the students' efforts. When a student is finished with this portion and the teacher approves the work (notices whether there are discernible patterns), that student is directed to use colored pencils to transfer those color patterns onto one side of grid paper. (The teacher should make sure students whose work has been approved do not share their work with others; they should color it and then turn the grid over.)

5. After a few of the students' work is approved and their pictures are penciled on their grids, the rest of the class is given extended time later in the day (or the following day) to complete their own matrices. Students are now brought back into the whole-class setting.

6. Pencils are put away and all eyes are directed to the overhead projector, where the teacher is standing with a blank matrix transparency (as seen in the appendix). The teacher begins calling on individual students to guess where the colors in one of the teacher's set-aside matrices are located (e.g., "Is C2 red?"). Students follow along at their desks with their interlocking colored cubes and the other (blank) side of their grid papers, trying to figure out the color patterns themselves.

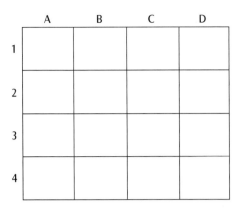

Figure 3.15

	A	B	C	D
1	Bl	R	Bk	G
2	Bl	R	Bk	G
3	Bl	R	Bk	G
4	Bl	R	Bk	G

Figure 3.16

	A	B	C	D
1	G	Bk	R	Bl
2	Bk	Bl	G	R
3	R	G	B1	Bk
4	Bl	R	Bk	G

Figure 3.17

7. The first student who figures out the teacher's pattern gets to come to the front of the room and lead the next puzzle game on the overhead using his or her "approved" matrix for class guesses.

Benefits

   a. A hands-on activity with full engagement possibility
   b. Patterns and colors—two powerful learning stimuli
   c. Identifying coordinates using "horizontal-vertical" pairings
   d. A high probability of some level of student direction

Extensions

   1. A larger grid
   2. Tie-ins with perfect squares (e.g., $4 \times 4 = 16$)
   3. A correct answer allows students to turn over that square on a new grid to reveal part of a picture to be identified
   4. Sequences of fill-in-the-blank color patterns
   5. Sequences of rhythm (music) or poetry (pentameter)
   6. Punnett Squares (genetic dominant/recessive tables) and probability

CRAZY QUILTS

(Grades 1–6) (Materials: Hundreds of 10-colored interlocking cubes)

NCTM Standard: Students will be able to apply transformations and use symmetry to analyze mathematical situations.

After giving each student access to hundreds of ten-color interlocking cubes, ask them to construct as many unique five-cube "letters" as they can.

The word "unique" is the key here—there are only 12 (listed below in Figure 3.18)—and students will come to understand that when they turn and flip their creations and recognize that theirs may be only a transformed version of an original.

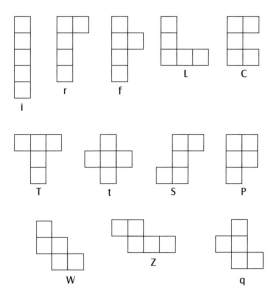

Figure 3.18

Extension 1: Students identify the letters that have horizontal line symmetry, vertical line symmetry, and/or rotational symmetry.

Next, each student is supplied with an 8-by-8 piece of grid paper in which the dimensions of each square on the grid match those of each block.

Extension 2: Students are asked to each make a two-dimensional "Crazy Quilt" with their 12-letter alphabets. They are to fit each piece inside the grid paper's boundaries (as in Figure 3.19—answers will vary).

Note: There will be four open squares (designated by the "O"). Ask your students if they can compute why that is ($64 - 12 \times 5 = 4$, by order of operations).

Extension 3: Students take a plain white piece of paper larger than their Crazy Quilts, slide it underneath, and label the bottom and left side axes as in Figure 3.20 (bigger than the 4-by-4 used in the "Guessing Matrix" piece—start by challenging your students to determine by just how much this matrix is bigger in perimeter [twice] and in area [four times]). (See the appendix for a blackline master.)

Students are then asked to identify the specific coordinates ("Letter-Number") for a handful of letters as preselected by the teacher.

Extension 4: Pair off students, and let them engage in a game of Battleship or of Cathedral (but with maybe 7 or 8 common letters allotted to each contestant.

Extension 5: Now students are asked to identify in words the transformation (flip, turn, and/or slide from the bottom left corner) that allowed them to fit into their Crazy Quilts a handful of letters as preselected by the teacher.

Extension 6: Students conduct an Internet search on two-dimensional molecular structures to determine if, indeed, only twelve such structures are known to exist in the field of chemistry.

Extension 7: Change the rules of your alphabet by taking away one block while allowing for "stacking" to create three-dimensional figures (there are 8 that are unique). Afterwards, ask each student to create either a 2-by-2-by-8 or a 2-by-4-by-4 rectangular solid (both of whose volumes must equal 32—another question to pose to the class, to which they might respond that there are 8 figures made up of 4 blocks each). See "How They Stack Up" in Chapter 4.

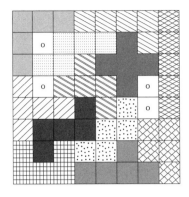

Figure 3.19

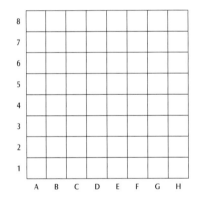

Figure 3.20

FOLD IT RIGHT THERE!

(Grades 5–8) (Materials: Listed below)

NCTM Standard: Students will be able to use visualization, spatial reasoning, and geometric modeling to solve problems.

One of the concerns I hear most often from workshop participants for whom I have presented standards-based lessons and activities is one of time—specifically, teachers are concerned that there simply is not enough time in the course of a school year to prepare students for statewide assessments, let alone introduce any of these cute little "add-ons" to an already-crowded lesson plan.

To address this issue, I argue that a teacher needs to create more time— "work smarter, not harder"—and weigh the benefits of a hands-on lesson that captures a wide range of mathematical concepts in a relatively brief sequence of directed instructional prompts. Besides the class covering more topics in less time, students themselves would benefit in three significant ways. They would:

- Be more engaged by utilizing another intelligence (tactile)
- Make more sense of math by "doing" and "discovering"
- Retain concepts longer (less repetition and less later review)

Materials: This activity starts with the teacher giving each student a cut-out, plain-paper circle of radius 10 cm. (See appendix for an 8-cm blackline master that may have to be enlarged for class copies.) Each student should also have a cm-base protractor and a sharp pencil.

The following pages describe how folding and turning a paper circle and performing simple drawing and labeling can help a student discover nearly three dozen basic geometric concepts (highlighted in bold) in one lesson:

Fewer Transitions = More Momentum = More Connections = Deeper Understanding

Figure 3.21

Step 1: Fold the bottom portion of the circle up and horizontally so that the arc of that portion of the circle passes through its center (Figure 3.21).

Step 2: Turn the paper a little bit to the left (counterclockwise), and fold the left portion of the circle up so that the arc of that portion of the circle passes through its center and the two arcs meet at a perfect bottom point (Figure 3.22).

Step 3: Fold the top portion of the circle down and horizontally so that the arc of that portion of the circle passes through its center. Opening the three arc-flaps you created and turning the paper back again a little bit to the right (clockwise) should yield the result shown in Figure 3.23.

Figure 3.22

Two transformations have already been demonstrated—**reflection** (the "flip" folding done three times) and **rotation** (slight "turning" done twice). And, in its folded-up form, the figure is actually two triangles back to back— one on a "perfect" side and one on the side with the three overlapping folds:

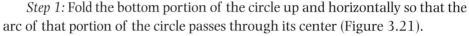

Two triangles × 180° each = 360° **circle** when the figure is unfolded.

The unfolded figure should consist of three parts of the circle (including **arcs**), each making a boundary along the sides of an **equilateral triangle**. Since each arc is congruent (perfect match) to the others, the circle is said to have been **trisected** (as shown in Figure 3.24): 360° ÷ 3 = 120° for each arc.

In addition, since the triangle is equilateral, it stands to reason that each angle must be congruent to the others, which allows for the triangle also to be classified as **equiangular**: 180° ÷ 3 = 60° for each angle.

Now, concentrate on any one angle of the triangle (Figure 3.25). The sides of the angle constitute **chords** of the circle, and the highlighted 120° arc is said to be **subtended** (cut off) by those chords. The **vertex** of the 60° angle lies right on the circle itself and is thus said to be **inscribed**.

Note: The measure of an inscribed angle is always one-half the measure of its subtended arc (in this case, $60° = \frac{1}{2} \times 120°$).

Step 4: Re-rotate the figure a little more to the left (counterclockwise), and, with your pencil and ruler (the base of the protractor), draw a chord (**diameter**) horizontally and right to left from the triangle's far right vertex through the center of the circle and over to the left side (i.e., through the three dots as shown in Figure 3.26).

The diameter **bisects** the circle: 360° ÷ 2 = 180° for each **semicircle**. It is also the longest chord of the circle, and it is equal in length to two **radii**.

Step 5: Think of the points on the circle that were just used to draw the diameter as **analog (face) clock** numbers 3:00 and 9:00. Momentarily disregard the radius drawn from the center of the circle to 9:00 and, instead, draw a new radius to 11:00 (Figure 3.27).

Both the radius to 3:00 and the one to 11:00 bisect the 60° angles of the original equilateral triangle: 60° ÷ 2 = 30°.

Now draw the chord connecting the 11:00 and 3:00 points on the circle as in Figure 3.28, thus creating an isosceles **triangle** (two sides are equal because they are both radii). The two angles opposite those equal sides of the isosceles triangle are referred to as **base angles**.

Note: Base angles of an isosceles triangle are always equal to each other.

The third angle of the isosceles triangle, the **vertex angle**, is found by adding the measures of the two base angles and subtracting from 180°: 180° − (30° + 30°) = 120°. However, we see in Figure 3.28 that 120° is also the measure of the subtended arc.

Note 1: The measure of any **central angle** in a circle (in this case, 120°) is equal to the measure of its subtended arc.

Note 2: While the triangle is isosceles (a "sides" classification), it could also be referred to as an **obtuse triangle** (an "angles" classification, in reference to its one angle which is greater than 90°).

Step 6: Now consider the 60° central angle in Figure 3.29. The two central angles thereby created above the diameter are in a 1:2 **ratio** (60° to 120°), they are **supplementary angles** (their sum is 180°), and they form a **straight angle** (180°). Drawing the

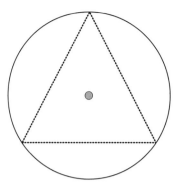

Figure 3.23

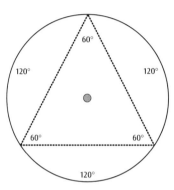

Figure 3.24

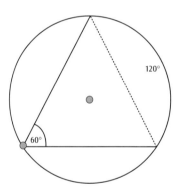

Figure 3.25

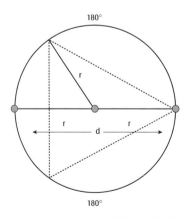

Figure 3.26

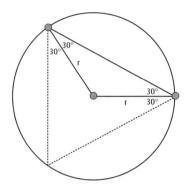

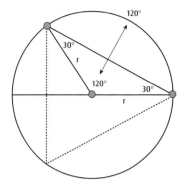

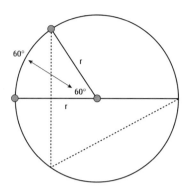

Figure 3.27   **Figure 3.28**   **Figure 3.29**

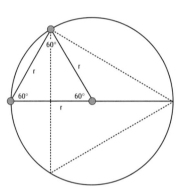

Figure 3.30

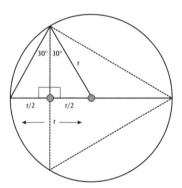

Figure 3.31

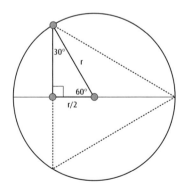

Figure 3.32

chord from 9:00 to 11:00 (Figure 3.30) turns out to be the same length as the radius (two 60° base angles)—meaning the new triangle is equiangular, equilateral, and **similar** (angles match and sides proportional) to the folded equilateral triangle in Figure 3.23.

Step 7: We can see that the smaller equilateral triangle is actually being bisected by one of the sides of the larger equilateral triangle.

This fold is a **perpendicular bisector**—bisecting the 60° angle at 11:00 (60° ÷ 2 = 30°), acting as an **altitude** to the radius (making two 90° angles), and bisecting the radius at its **midpoint** ($r \div 2 = \frac{r}{2}$) (Figure 3.31).

Step 8: The perpendicular bisector creates two **congruent triangles** (the one to the left of the fold can literally be folded right on top of the one to the right of the fold).

Choosing just one of the triangles, it may be described as either **right** (angle classified) or **scalene** (sides classified). The two **acute angles** (those less than 90°) are **complementary** to each other because their sum is 90°.

Note: As shown in Figure 3.32, the sides opposite the 30° angle (the shorter **leg**) and the 90° angle (the **hypotenuse**) are labeled $\frac{r}{2}$ and r, respectively. Their ratio is 1:2 and should actually measure 5 cm and 10 cm.

Extensions

Find the length of the longer leg (across from the 60° angle).

Use that triangle to determine basic sine, cosine, and tangent ratios.

Find the areas of both the smaller and larger equilateral triangles.

Summary of Terms: "Fold It Right There!"

Can you recall all 35 of the following terms from the lesson we just did together?

acute angle
altitude
analog clock
arc
base angles
bisection
central angle
chord
complementary angles
congruent triangles
diameter
equiangular triangle
equilateral triangle
hypotenuse
inscribed angle
isosceles triangle
leg
midpoint

obtuse triangle
perpendicular bisector
radius
ratio
reflection
right triangle
rotation
scalene triangle
semicircle
similar triangles
straight angle
subtended arc
sum of a circle's angles
sum of a triangle's angles
supplementary angles
trisection
vertex angle

Measurement 4

A high-quality instructional program in Grades K–8 will enable all students to:

- Understand measurable attributes of objects and the units, systems, and processes of measurement; and

- Apply appropriate techniques, tools, and formulas to determine measurements.

OVERVIEW

In many ways, measurement is the true essence of mathematics—and of our existence. Note how the numbers we use to measure something in the present give us meaning because we are able to make a comparison based upon a relative scale of measurements that were established previously.

For example, suppose you are a student and receive a grade of 48 on a test. Egad! This would not be a very good grade to get if the relative scale was 100 points ($\frac{48}{100} = 48\%$). But, should the relative scale be 50 points, it would turn out that scoring 48 out of 50 ($\frac{48}{50} = 96\%$) translates into a solid "A."

Think about how often we use measuring against an established scale in our everyday conversations with others: "How fast was I going, Officer?" "How long was that putt?" "How many calories are in one serving of this stuff?" Or, "What part of this credit card bill should we pay this month?" It would be fair to say that we measure and compare quantities pretty much on a constant basis.

So, the next time you hear someone utter the tired bromide, "Well, you know, I was never really very good at math," the issues that truly impact them may be real-world but are *still* math-related—driving, competing, diet, or money. Some questions of measurement for us to ponder in the upcoming introduction "How So?" will be How Fast? How Far? How Big? (which includes the original TI-73 program application **ACUANGLS**), and How Many?

"I Scream . . . You Scream . . ." is printed with permission from Kathy A. Welch-Martin, National Board Certified Teacher, Early Adolescence Mathematics.

The rest of the chapter comprises three activities, the last two of which combine yet another original TI-73 program (**RECTSURA**) with three-dimensional modeling and pattern considerations ("How They Stack Up"). Success with the first activity ("I Scream . . . You Scream . . .") can instantly be measured by the quality and taste of ice cream made in class. Whether or not directions were closely followed and measuring methods were accurate will be obvious.

HOW SO?

The four scenarios that make up this introduction demonstrate the power of mathematics in that none of the measurements performed below are direct (like measuring one's height or counting the number of tickets sold to a play).

Rather, *indirect* measurement—by its very nature more of a calculated guess—applies various mathematical tools to situations that otherwise would be difficult, if not impossible, to measure and verify firsthand.

Scenario 1: If the current world record time in the men's 100-meter dash is 9.79 seconds, how fast would that be in miles per hour?

Dimensional Analysis is an application of a series of scale fractions that are multiplied to reach a desired result (Chapter 1: Numbers and Operations):

100 m. / 9.79 sec. × 3.281 ft. / 1 m. × 1 mile / 5280 ft. × 3600 sec. / 1 hr. = 22.85 mph or (rounded) = **almost 23 miles per hour.** (Wow!)

Follow-Up Question: How fast does a world-class women's marathoner—covering 26.2 miles in two hours and 25 minutes—actually run in miles per hour?

Answer: No heavy lifting required! Simply divide 26.2 miles by 2.42 hours on a calculator and get 10.8 mph or (rounded) **almost 11 miles per hour.**

The marathoner's speed is almost half the sprinter's speed—and is maintained for almost two and a half hours! Although much different in their respective anaerobic and aerobic strengths, both runners are most impressive!

Scenario 2: Given an inflated splash/wading pool for young children, can you tell how far it would be from one end of the pool to the other without directly measuring?

(A word of caution: If you *must* fill the pool, do *not* use water.)

Indirect measurement is what a surveying crew actually performs measuring across, say, a lake, and your class may enjoy doing the same on a small scale (Figure 4.1 with the big circle represents the pool that we will assume to be 3 feet across).

Materials: One large flag (the empty point in Figures 4.1, 4.2, and 4.3), four small flags (colored-in points), string and scissors, and a regular ruler.

As shown in Figure 4.2, the first small flag at Home and the one large flag directly due north across the pool (x = the circle's diameter).

Set a second small flag 2 feet farther north and string the 2-foot distance.

Turn left (west), set a third small flag 4 feet from where you just were, and string the 4-foot distance.

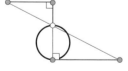

Figure 4.1

Return Home, set the fourth small flag 6 feet due east, and string the 6-foot distance.

(Two pairs of small flags—NW and E, N and Home—should be aligned with the large flag.)

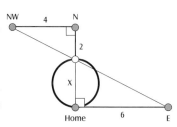

Figure 4.2

The teacher has several instructional options available (Chapter 2: Algebra, Chapter 3: Geometry), but any one of them should include a demonstration of the half-turn swing of the upper triangle into the lower one (Figure 4.3):

$$\text{If } \frac{2}{4} = \frac{x}{6}, \text{ then } x = 3.$$

Scenario 3: With a protractor, determine the measures of both acute (less than 90°) angles of some given right triangles. Check your answers for accuracy with the original program written for the TI-73 graphing calculator that follows.

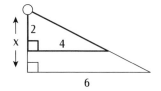

Figure 4.3

Before starting, consider trying a little logical reasoning with your more mature students using Figure 4.4.

For any triangle ABC, the sum of the measures of the three angles = 180°; that is, $A + B + C = 180°$. If the triangle is a right triangle, let's call the measure of angle C = 90°. So, by substitution, $A + B + 90° = 180°$. Subtracting 90° from both sides of the equation, we are left with $A + B = 90°$. Since the protractor measures only *positive* angles, both A and B by themselves must be less than 90° (thus, both are acute).

Students were given protractors, centimeter rulers, and three cutout right triangles of various sizes and reached consensus with the following results:

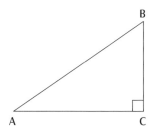

Figure 4.4

	Leg AC	Leg BC	Hypotenuse AB	Angle A	Angle B
Triangle 1	8	6	10	37	53°
Triangle 2	7	9	12	49°	36°
Triangle 3	12.5	21.6	25	60°	30°

Oops! Solving problems is a little clearer for students when they recall the four-step process, "U-PL-EX-L": Understand, PLan, EXecute, and . . . LOOK BACK! Angles A and B are acute in the answers above, to be sure, but A+B must also = 90° (making what mathematicians refer to as **complementary angles**).

Triangles 1 and 3 are good to go! But, Triangle 2, not so fast!

Students should also be reminded that any triangle ABC is considered a right triangle if and only if $AC^2 + BC^2 = AB^2$. For the lengths of the sides in Triangle 2, $7^2 + 9^2 = 49 + 81 = 130 \neq 12^2$ (which is 144, not 130).

Conclusion: Triangle 2 was never a right triangle to begin with (and, if students measure angle C with their protractors, they should get 85°, not 90°).

By the way, there's method to the madness in the choices for the three sides (12.5, 21.6, and 25 cm) in Triangle 3. If you recall the paper folding we did back in the introduction of Chapter 3, the triangle we *would* have created had we made a fold with our very first move has those very dimensions (Figure 4.5).

Question: Notice in the answers in the above chart that the acute angles for Triangle 3 are 60° and 30°, making the triangle a "30–60–90" right triangle. Can you reason *why* those acute angles *have* to be 60° and 30°?

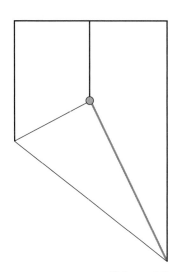

Figure 4.5

CALCULATOR APPLICATION (GRADES 7–8)

Finding the Measures of the Two Acute Angles of a Right Triangle

The following original program, ACUANGLS, is a real challenge to enter into the TI-73 in that it is long and contains lots of punctuation. None of it is especially complicated—it just takes time and attention to detail, with a nice payoff when executed.

```
PROGRAM:ACUANGLS
:ClrScreen
:Disp "FIND_MEAS
URES_OF"
:Disp "THE_TWO_
ACUTE"
:Disp "ANGLES_OF
_A"
:Disp "RIGHT_TRI
ANGLE"
:Pause
:ClrScreen
:Disp "LABEL_THE_
RIGHT"
:Disp "ANGLE_=_C_
and_"
:Disp "HYPOTENUSE
_=_AB"
:Pause
:ClrScreen
:AC -> X
:BC -> Y
:AB -> Z
```

```
:Disp "SIDE_LENG
THS:"
:Disp "_"
:Input "LEG_AC_
=_," X
:Disp "_"
:Input "LEG_BC_
=_," Y
:Disp "_"
:Input "HYPOT._AB_
=_," Z
:Pause
:ClrScreen
:Disp "THE_ANGLES
_ARE:"
:Disp "_"
:Disp "_A_=_,"
round(sin⁻¹(Y / Z),0)
:Disp "_"
:Disp "_and_B_=_,"
round(sin⁻¹(X / Z),0)
```

```
:Pause
:ClrScreen
:If round(sin⁻¹(X / Z), 0)
  + round(sin⁻¹
(Y / Z), 0) ≠ 90
:Then
:Disp "AC²_+_BC²_
≠_AB²"
:Disp "_"
:Disp "PLEASE_CH
ECK"
:Disp "YOUR_WORK
_AND"
:Disp "TRY_AGAIN!"
:Pause
```

Note: For the Erase Phase and for directions on how to either reset or escape the following, please refer to the MULTFRAX program developed in Chapter 1: Numbers and Operations.

Input and Output for Triangles 1 and 2 follow. The reader is encouraged to input the legs and hypotenuse for Triangle 3 without assistance to see if the output of 60° and 30° is indeed obtained.

Your Input	**Output**
PRGM	
Scroll down (Arrow Down) to ACUANGLS	
ENTER	prgmACUANGLS
ENTER	FIND MEASURES OF THE TWO ACUTE ANGLES OF A RIGHT TRIANGLE
ENTER	LABEL THE RIGHT ANGLE = C and HYPOTENUSE = AB
ENTER 8 ENTER 6 ENTER 10 ENTER	SIDE LENGTHS: LEG AC = 8 LEG BC = 6 HYPOT. AB = 10

ENTER	THE ANGLES ARE:
	A =
	               37
	and B =
	               53

ENTER ENTER ENTER	prgmACUANGLS Done
ENTER 7 ENTER 9 ENTER 12 ENTER	SIDE LENGTHS: LEG AC = 7 LEG BC = 9 HYPOT. AB = 12

ENTER	THE ANGLES ARE:
	A =
	               49
	and B =
	               36

ENTER	$AC^2 + BC^2 \neq AB^2$ PLEASE CHECK YOUR WORK AND TRY AGAIN!
ENTER	prgmACUANGLS Done

Scenario 4: "How are they biting today?" This upstate New York region of the United States where I live is truly blessed with some of the most numerous sources of fresh water in the world—two of the five Great Lakes (Erie and Ontario), a beautiful and powerful river shared with our great Canadian friends (Niagara), a swathe of picturesque inland jewels (the Finger Lakes), and countless feeder streams and creeks. So, it's not uncommon to hear questions about fishing up our way.

It's also not uncommon for children to wonder how many fish reside within a certain body of water. (One could drain an area and actually count, but doing so is certainly not very practical—not to mention a bad idea for the fish.) And some adults, such as the state's Department of Environmental Conservation (DEC), have more than a passing interest in their efforts to closely monitor various species of fish for health and public safety.

So, a restocking process has been developed whereby a predetermined amount of a certain fish (e.g., lake trout) is farm raised, tagged, and released into the water after the fishing season has ended. During a fishing derby the following year, licensed anglers bring their catches to a weigh station where DEC members record the percentage of the take that is tagged—the lower the percentage, the more successful the process is for species maintenance.

The mathematics involved is quite straightforward (Chapter 2: Algebra, Chapter 5: Data Analysis and Probability). It involves this basic proportion:

Sample ÷ Population = Sample ÷ Population

The left side represents the tagged and released lake trout (sample) and the unknown number of trout (x) estimated to be in the lake (population). The right side contains the numbers from the following year's fishing derby—the number of tagged trout (sample) out of the entire catch (population).

Let's say that 200 lake trout are tagged and released and the following year 500 trout are caught, 25 of which have tags ($\frac{25}{500}$ = a percentage of 5%). The estimated total number of trout in the lake would be: $200 \div x = 25 \div 500 \rightarrow$ x = about 4,000 lake trout (healthy supply).

Now let's say that the same number of farm-raised trout are released, but of the 500 trout that are caught the following year, 100 have tags ($\frac{100}{500}$ = a percentage of 20%). The estimated total number of trout in the lake would now be: $200 \div x = 100 \div 500 \rightarrow$ x = about 1,000 lake trout (a much lower supply).

In a situation like this, the DEC may move to step up its repopulation program while at the same time shortening or even temporarily suspending the lake trout fishing season in these waters. And the effect of licensing cannot be overemphasized—besides being the best way to regulate the sport (fairness in competition), it also offers some degree of deterrence to those who fish out of season (and disrupt critical reproduction patterns).

I SCREAM . . . YOU SCREAM . . .

Guest Contributor: Kathy Welch-Martin

(Grades 4–6) (Materials: Please refer to the recipe)

NCTM Standard: Students will be able to understand measurable attributes of objects and the units, systems, and processes of measurement.

Suppose you work the day shift in the quality control department of an ice cream manufacturer. The person who works the night shift in your common work area has left you the company recipe for Marvelous Mustang Ice Cream along with a set of measuring utensils.

First, the recipe:

Marvelous Mustang Ice Cream

Get two different sized resealable freezer bags. In the larger freezer bag, place 1 to 2 cups of crushed ice and 5 tablespoons of salt.

In the smaller freezer bag, place the following ingredients:

1/2 cup Half 'n Half
2 tablespoons sugar
1/2 teaspoon vanilla extract

Tightly seal the smaller freezer bag, and then place it in the larger bag with the ice and the salt. Tightly seal the larger bag.

Shake the bags for 10 to 15 minutes until your ice cream has reached its desired consistency. Taste test with a spoon, and then enjoy.

However, you have a problem! The measuring utensils that were left for you—a 1/4 teaspoon, a 1 teaspoon, and a 2 oz. cup—do not match the measurements that you need to make your Marvelous Mustang Ice Cream.

After an intensive search around the manufacturing plant, you managed to find the following note card:

Remember:
3 teaspoons (tsp. or t.) = 1 tablespoon (tbsp. or T.)
2 ounces (oz.) = 1/4 cup

Using the information provided and the utensils that you have, you are to prepare a batch of ice cream. When you have reached the desired consistency, completely fill out your Quality Control Report (see blackline masters in appendix) and file it with your department manager (your teacher).

Then, if you've calculated and measured correctly, you'll enjoy the results of your ice cream making efforts! (Note: An answer key for the chart follows.)

Guest contributor Kathy A. Welch-Martin has been a mathematics teacher for the past twenty-five years at Wainwright Middle School in Lafayette, Indiana. She is a National Board Certified Teacher in Early Adolescence Mathematics and was the 1999 Indiana recipient of the Presidential Award for Excellence in Secondary Mathematics Teaching. She has worked on a variety of National Science Foundation research grants through Purdue University and Indiana University and has collaborated on educational projects with NASA Glenn Research Center in Cleveland, Ohio.

Ingredient	Amount Needed	Measuring Utensil Used	Amount Used (Show Calculations)
Example: Chocolate Syrup	$\frac{3}{4}$ teaspoon	$\frac{1}{4}$ teaspoon	$\frac{3}{4} \div \frac{1}{4} = \frac{3}{4} \times \frac{4}{1}$ $= $ Three $\frac{1}{4}$ teaspoons
Ice	For 1 cup → For 2 cups →	2 oz. $= \frac{1}{4}$ cup	$1 \div \frac{1}{4} = $ Four $\frac{1}{4}$ cups $2 \div \frac{1}{4} = $ Eight $\frac{1}{4}$ cups
Salt	5 Tablespoons	1 tsp. $= \frac{1}{3}$ T.	$5 \div \frac{1}{3} = 5 \times \frac{3}{1}$ $= $ Fifteen teaspoons
Half 'n Half	$\frac{1}{2}$ cup	$\frac{1}{4}$ cup	$\frac{1}{2} \div \frac{1}{4} = \frac{1}{2} \times \frac{4}{1}$ $= $ Two $\frac{1}{4}$ cups
Sugar	2 Tablespoons	1 T. $=$ 3 tsp.	2×3 $= $ Six teaspoons
Vanilla	$\frac{1}{2}$ teaspoon	$\frac{1}{4}$ teaspoon	$\frac{1}{2} \div \frac{1}{4} = \frac{1}{2} \times \frac{4}{1}$ $= $ Two $\frac{1}{4}$ teaspoons

HOW THEY STACK UP

(Grades K–8) (Materials: Hundreds of 10-color interlocking cubes, two worksheets, pencil; optional: A class set of TI-73 graphing calculators)

NCTM Standard: Students will be able to apply appropriate techniques, tools, and formulas to determine measurements.

This wide-ranging, hands-on activity has potential benefits for students in any grade or at any ability level. A regular classroom would need a *huge* supply of same-size interlocking cubes in a variety of colors (the author's favorite type comes shipped in bulks of 1,000, or 100 each in ten available colors). Believe it or not, upwards of 3,000 cubes would work well here.

Note: Not every item mentioned below applies to every student. That being said, there is still a lot of ground to be covered (some 16 different activities, numbered below), so allow 3 to 5 days.

1. A **polyhedron** is a three-dimensional figure (in space) that is bounded by polygons (**faces**). A **regular polyhedron**, then, would have all of its faces congruent (just like a regular polygon has all of its sides congruent).

In the case of a cube (resembling a die we might use for a board game), it has six congruent faces (all squares) and is formally known as a **hexahedron.** There are five so-called regular polyhedra, but a cube is easily the most recognizable of the group.

2. If students each take one cube they will notice that, besides the six square faces, there are also eight corners (**vertices**) and twelve line segments (**edges**).

There exists a really interesting formula, known as **Euler's Formula**, that connects the number of vertices (V), the number of faces (F), and the number of edges (E): $V + F = E + 2$. For the cube, then, $8 + 6 = 12 + 2$, or $14 = 14$.

Students with an interest in pursuing this relationship are urged to access information from the Internet and acquaint themselves more closely with the other four regular polyhedra in order to see the formula at work.

3. There have been some cooperative learning opportunities purposely worked into this activity, but, as the ancient Romans would say, *caveat emptor* (which is Latin for "let the buyer beware"). Cooperative learning has the potential for some powerful teaching . . . *but only if everyone cooperates!*

Ask students to each go to the cube container (in an orderly fashion) and take nine more cubes back to their seats. The choice of color does not matter. (How many cubes does each child now have? $1 + 9 = 10$.) Expand on the arithmetic operation possibilities. Students could lay all ten cubes in front of them and the teacher could give a series of hands-on instructions to the class, calling on students one at a time to give answers.

For example: "Take five away" ($10 - 5 = 5$), "Put three back" ($5 + 3 = 8$), "Divide what's in front of you in half" ($8 \div 2 =$ two groups of 4), "Take one away from both groups" ($4 - 1 =$ two groups of 3), "Make one more group just like the two groups you have in front of you. What do you have now?" (three groups of $3 = 3 \times 3 = 9$), "What do you need to get back to ten?" ($9 + 1 = 10$).

This is a great opportunity for you to be creative!

4. (Here is another cooperative part: At this point, each child has ten cubes. Have students (again, in an orderly fashion) each put three of their cubes back into the cube container and return to their seats. (How many cubes does each child now have? $10 - 3 = 7$.)

Now, let's suppose that there are twenty students in your classroom. Before the class convenes, the teacher preselects twenty cubes—two each of the ten colors available (one cube per student is known as a **one-to-one correspondence**)—and, having already placed them in a small paper bag, moves around the room and asks each child to pick one cube out of the bag. (How many cubes does each child now have? $7 + 1 = 8$.)

That one cube the child picks becomes that student's key color. The student then looks (again, in an orderly fashion) for his or her partner in the classroom, and those two same-key color-cube students get together and begin working. (How many cubes does each pairing of students now have? $8 + 8 = 16$.)

5. What each partnership needs at this point, though, is for all **16** of their cubes to be in their key color. Each partnership needs to get rid of any other colors while holding onto their key color (*major* cooperation required at this stage) by trading with the other partnerships.

The trading process with other students now commences (again, in an orderly fashion). For example, suppose Partners A are looking for the color Orange. When the teacher starts the process by calling on them, they show the class that they'd like to get rid of, say, the color Blue and trade it for Orange. If Partners B (whose key color is Blue) have an Orange cube(s) in their possession that they would like to unload, they raise their hands. Partners A and B then perform the trade (always one-for-one).

Then, it becomes Partners B's turn, showing the rest of the class they have, say, Yellow to trade for Blue. If Partners C (whose key color is Yellow) have a Blue cube(s) in their possession that they would like to unload, they raise *their* hands. Partners B and C then perform the Yellow-for-Blue trade. Then it becomes Partners C's turn, and so on, until each partnership has all 16 of their cubes in their key color. (For any partnership still short, the teacher finishes the process with orderly trading from the cube container.)

6. Until now, the cubes have remained separated. They will now begin to be connected (and the mathematics will really get going as a result).

Have each partnership take all 16 of their cubes and snap them together so that they make one long "snake." Then, give them copies of the chart below (Figure 4.6), (see appendix for a blackline master), and ask them to perform some counts (measurements), beginning with the length ($L = 16$) and the width ($W = 1$) of their snakes.

L	W	Perimeter (Add Edges)	Area (Add Faces)

Figure 4.6

The next count for each partnership is to determine, laying the snake flat on the desk, how many edges it takes to "go once around" (perimeter P = 34). (The teacher may wish to have students use tracing paper here.) After that is accomplished, the last count is to determine how many of the snake's faces are actually in contact with the desk, or "face down" (area A = 16).

7. (More cooperation.) The teacher will now involve the class in five related tasks:

    a. Divide the class in half on either side of the room.

    b. Have a little fun with the chart (Figure 4.7). Ask the entire class to figure out what might happen to numbers in the first column (L), which are cut in half at the same time numbers in the second column (W) are doubled. Put the results in the chart.

    c. Ask each partnership on both sides of the room to break their snakes in half (each piece 16 ÷ 2 = 8 cubes), snap the two pieces together (Figure 4.8), and measure the length (L = 8) and width (W = 2).

    d. Ask the partnerships on one side of the room to go one step further and break their "8-by-2's" in half once more (each double piece 8 ÷ 2 = 4), snap those two pieces together (Figure 4.9), and measure this new configuration's length (L = 4) and width (W = 4).

    e. Have partnerships on both sides of the room determine "How many edges?" (perimeter) and "How many faces down?" (area) for their once-split or twice-split figures. Put the results in the chart, and be sure the information found on both sides of the room is shared (Figure 4.10).

8. Here's a perfect example of why the author's Rule 1 ("'Tis better to do math than to receive it") is so critical to student understanding.

Let's study the chart we just completed, and let's *think!* First, as our eyes scan downward notice that the last column (Area) contains the same number (the constant = 16). Notice also that the first two columns (Length and Width) contain numbers that, when read across and multiplied, also equal 16.

It would appear, then, that **Length × Width = Area.**

The students weren't told this or asked to take it verbatim from some textbook, write it down in their notebooks, or (heaven forbid) *memorize* some meaningless drivel. No,

L	W	Perimeter (Add Edges)	Area (Add Faces)
16	1	34	16
8	2		
4	4		

Figure 4.7

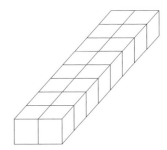

Figure 4.8

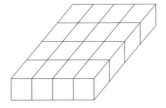

Figure 4.9

L	W	Perimeter (Add Edges)	Area (Add Faces)
16	1	34	16
8	2	20	16
4	4	16	16

Figure 4.10

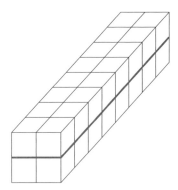

Figure 4.11

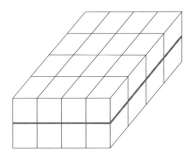

Figure 4.12

L	W	H	Perimeter (Add Edges)	Area (Add Faces)

Figure 4.13

L	W	H	Perimeter (Add Edges)	Area (Add Faces)
16	1	1		

Figure 4.14

they can actually *see* evidence that it works the way a teacher or a textbook says it should. This is much more powerful, much more interesting, and has a much better chance of longer student retention. It's called TEACHING!

One more concept is at work in the chart, albeit a bit subtler. Even though the Area column is frozen at 16, the values in the Perimeter column decrease as our eyes scan downward. It turns out that, given a constant area, the shortest perimeter occurs when the four-sided figure is a square (like the 4-by-4 figure made by the "twice-splitter" partnerships in the room).

In the real world, this translates into lower costs for any sort of enclosure (fencing, baseboard) that a consumer with a specific area in mind might make.

9. Now, pair partnerships together to make groups of four students each. The ideal scenario would be to pair partnerships who have made 8-by-2's (once-splitters) so that these new groups could snap colored 8-by-2's on top of differently colored 8-by-2's to create models of rectangular solids (boxes) resembling Figure 4.11 (an 8-by-2-by-2).

The same should be done with pairs of 4-by-4 creating partners (twice-splitters) so that these new groups are able to snap together 4-by-4-by-2 models of rectangular solids resembling Figure 4.12.

Note: The reason for having partnerships use one color for making their models is to illustrate very neatly the idea of horizontal-plane symmetry. The reader is invited to check for vertical-plane symmetry as well.

It is also interesting to consider *rotational* symmetry. If two lines meet at a common point (rotational *point* symmetry for two-dimensional figures), then it follows that two planes meet along a common line (creating rotational *line* symmetry for three-dimensional figures).

If one can visualize boring a small tunnel through the middle of the front face of either figure above (and exiting in the middle of the respective back face), then "spinning" either model (if all its cubes were the *same* color) 180° on the "rod" inserted through that front-to-back central tunnel has no effect. (Another rod from side to side could also be inserted with like results.)

10. Let the focus now be on how many cubes (**volume**) and how many total faces on all six sides (**surface area**) comprise the two types of models around the room. Results are entered on Figure 4.13; a blackline master appears in the appendix.

a. After asking to have those rectangular solid models put aside for a few minutes, now have one student from each four-person group come to the cube container (there should be only five or six students doing so) and take any new color of 16 more cubes back to his or her group.

Each group snaps together a brand new 16-cube "snake," and the teacher emphasizes the presence of three dimensions (edges) with this snake: L = 16, W = 1, and H (height) = 1 (Figure 4.14).

b. Have the groups analyze their new snakes and measure (count) how many cubes (V = 16) and how many total faces (SA = 66) there are.

Then, in order to collect more V and SA data, have the groups first measure the effect of breaking their new snakes in half and then snapping the halves back together (8-by-2-by-1) and then repeating the process with another break in half and snapping quarters together (4-by-4-by-1) (Figure 4.15).

The chart also allows for each group to transition and to collect V and SA data for their own rectangular solid models (the 8-by-2-by-2 or the 4-by-4-by-2 boxes) that were constructed previously. All results should be shared around the room and subsequently entered (as is shown in Figure 4.16).

L	W	H	Volume (Add Cubes)	Surface Area (Add Faces)
16	1	1	16	66
8	2	1		
4	4	1		

Figure 4.15

L	W	H	Volume (Add Cubes)	Surface Area (Add Faces)
16	1	1	16	66
8	2	1	16	52
8	2	2	32	72
4	4	1	16	48
4	4	2	32	64

Figure 4.16

11. In studying this latest chart we just completed, we notice three trends that lead to some interesting ideas:

For one, an extension of a previous discovery we made, we can see that the first three columns (length, width, and height) contain numbers that, when read across and multiplied, equal the number in the volume column.

We can conclude, then, that **Length × Width × Height = Volume.** (There will be some more thoughts expressed about this formula in the next section.)

Second, much like before, dimensionality (this time with constant height and volume) is interesting to compare. Note that, for the two entries reading across where H = 2 and V = 32 (the two rectangular solid models groups have made), the 4-by-4-by-2 model has a *smaller* surface area than the 8-by-2-by-2.

This might not seem like a big deal, but real-world companies involved with any kind of packaging are able to fit more product into shipping boxes or containers where Length and Width are closer (or, in the case of the 4-by-4-by-2 model, equal) to each other. Hence, those companies stay more competitive because they have *minimized* their packaging and shipping costs.

Third, students with either model before them should be able to make physical affirmations of the jumps in surface areas reflected in the chart. Those with the 8-by-2-by-2 models have two differently colored layers of 8-by-2-by-1's and count their model's increase in surface area by 20 (from 52 to 72). Those with the 4-by-4-by-2 models have two differently colored layers of 4-by-4-by-1's and count their model's increase in surface area by 16 (from 48 to 64).

12. Let's explore the concept of "layering" a little more closely. Compare the formulas for **Area (L × W)** and **Volume (L × W × H).** Clearly, the difference is in the inclusion of height H, taking a rectangle (L × W) and adding layers of that same rectangle on top of it (H = the number of layers).

The same holds true when we compare formulas for the area of a circle (πr^2) and the volume of a cylinder ($\pi r^2 \times h$). Think of a cylinder as a stack of CDs or of pancakes—nothing more than circles put one on top of the other.

13. The original program, RECTSURA, is a means for teachers to infuse technology into the classroom so that students may check answers to questions involving surface areas (SA) of six-sided boxes. The program will verify SA = 72 for the 8-by-2-by-2 model and SA = 64 for the 4-by-4-by-2 model.

14. A brief scan of the RECTSURA program itself will reveal the formula most commonly used to find the surface area of a rectangular solid:

Surface Area = 2 × Length × Width + 2 × Length × Height + 2 × Width × Height

However important it might be for students to know this formula, it is even more important that they understand how the formula actually *works*.

It turns out that the repeating number 2 represents the essence of the formula. Recall earlier in this unit that the rectangular solid models that were constructed had both horizontal- and vertical-plane symmetries as well as rotational line symmetry.

With the models in front of them to analyze, students are invited to THINK about the six sides of their models. Pairs of sides are symmetrically congruent—the top and bottom **(2 × L × W)** , the two sides **(2 × L × H),** and the front and back **(2 × W × H).** Add up those results, and the formula becomes obvious.

15. One student from each four-person group is now asked to return (in an orderly fashion) the 16 cubes her or his group just used to the cube container (leaving the models of the rectangular solids made earlier intact and still with each group).

Their mission now is to take from the cube container 32 cubes—4 apiece of 8 different colors (the remaining colors not used in constructing their solid models). Members of the entire group will now engage in making 4-cube *letters*

of a two- and three-dimensional alphabet comprised of the eight letters in
Figures 4.17–4.24:

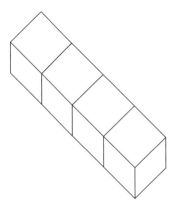

Figure 4.17

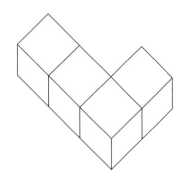

Figure 4.18

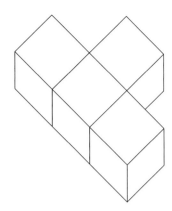

Figure 4.19

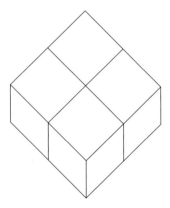

Figure 4.20

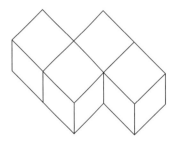

Figure 4.21

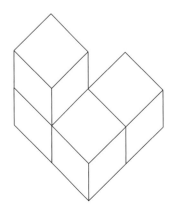

Figure 4.22

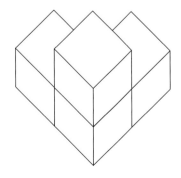

Figure 4.23

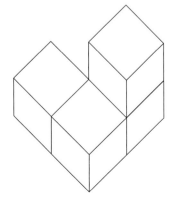

Figure 4.24

CALCULATOR APPLICATION (GRADES 5–8)

Surface Area of a Rectangular Solid

Note: For both the Erase Phase and for directions on how to either reset or escape the following, please refer to the MULTFRAX program introduction section of Chapter 1: Numbers and Operations.

```
PROGRAM:RECTSURA              :Input "LENGTH_=_,"L
:ClrScreen                    :Disp "_"
:Disp "FIND_SURFACE"          :Input "WIDTH_=_,"W
:Disp "AREA_OF_A"             :Disp "_"
:Disp "RECTANGULAR"           :Input "HEIGHT_=_,"H
:Disp "SOLID_(BOX)"           :Pause
:Pause                        :ClrScreen
:ClrScreen                    :Disp "SURFACE_
:Disp "DIMEN                  AREA_="
SIONS?_:"                     :Disp 2 × L × W + 2 × L × H + 2 × W × H
:Disp "_"                     :Pause
```

Your Input	Output
PRGM Scroll down (Arrow Down) to RECTSURA ENTER	prgmRECTSURA
ENTER	FIND SURFACE AREA OF A RECTANGULAR SOLID (BOX)
ENTER 8 ENTER 2 ENTER 2 ENTER	DIMENSIONS? : LENGTH = 8 WIDTH = 2 HEIGHT = 2
ENTER	SURFACE AREA = 72
ENTER ENTER	prgmRECTSURA Done
ENTER 4 ENTER 4 ENTER 2 ENTER	DIMENSIONS? : LENGTH = 4 WIDTH = 4 HEIGHT = 2
ENTER	SURFACE AREA = 64
ENTER	prgmRECTSURA Done

The teacher may wish to have models of each of the letters available for the students to use during their construction (guided discovery) or may opt to give the students verbal instructions or hints *only* (creative discovery).

16. Either way, the endgame for each group is to build all eight letters and then use them to recreate the rectangular solid they have already built! This is a really interesting cooperative learning activity to observe and enjoy.

In fact, the teacher may wish to subdivide each of the groups (back to partnerships) and, within each group, direct one partnership to recreate the 8-by-2-by-2 model and the other partnership to recreate the 4-by-4-by-2 model. Those partnerships who hang in there and keep plugging away with various flips-turns-slides before they ultimately achieve success will gain a real sense of accomplishment—a fun character and self-esteem builder for all!

Data Analysis and Probability 5

A high-quality instructional program in Grades K–8 will enable students to:

- Formulate questions that can be addressed with data and collect, organize, and display relevant data in order to answer them;
- Select and use appropriate statistical methods to analyze data;
- Develop and evaluate inferences and predictions that are based on data; and
- Understand and apply basic concepts of probability.

OVERVIEW

The title of the introduction, "Even the Odds," is a double entendre speaking not only to the even-odd number dichotomy but also to the concept of probability and the major part it plays in the last of the five content standards.

As a brief aside, textbook editors frequently place the unit or units on probability and data analysis (statistics) toward the end of their textbooks—almost as if to relegate the two closely related concepts to a math purgatory of sorts. Truth be told and given the flexibility to do so, many math teachers would prefer to expose their students to probability and statistics much earlier in the school year—somewhere between fundamental/review units on numbers and those on measurement (with geometry and algebra positioned later).

The reasons are quite simple. Probability is defined as a fraction (the number of desired outcomes divided by the number of possible outcomes) and thus is a perfect follow-up to number fraction work. Statistics is defined as the collection, organization, and interpretation of data—taking numbers (hopefully generated by the students themselves) and performing various operations on them such as averages (again a fraction) and a host of visual graphs.

In this spirit, yours truly is finishing this book with a flourish. "Even the Odds," for one, uses several arguments to approach the posing of a hypothetical in-class question—probability, algebra, random numbers, a tree diagram, a binary operation system matrix, and even one final original TI-73 graphing calculator program (**ODDOREVN**).

Four additional activities follow: "Read More About It!" examines the connections between the daily newspaper and math, "Living Graphs" highlights cooperative learning through whole-class and small-group activities, "Fire and Ice" looks at the three different phases of water (solid, liquid, and gas), and "Games of Chance" puts students and probability into motion with some athletic events.

EVEN THE ODDS

In a recent visit to a middle-school math classroom, I observed a teacher discussing with students the patterns inherent in adding various combinations of odd and even numbers. The point of the discussion was to illustrate how the concept of probability works.

Three cases using natural numbers were laid out for the class to ponder:

1. An even number + an even number = an **Even** number

2. An odd number + an odd number = an **Even** number

3. An odd number + an even number = an **Odd** number

Since probability is defined in fraction form as the number of desired outcomes divided by the number of possible outcomes, the teacher concluded (and the students agreed with the assessment) that, given two random numbers, the probability that their sum will be odd is $\frac{1}{3}$.

To buttress that assertion, the class was then led through a logical argument based on algebraic reasoning. Start with any number, x. Whether that number is even or odd, doubling that number (2x) will create an even number. And, thus, adding 1 to that new number (2x + 1) will create an odd number.

Now, return to the three cases mentioned earlier, and write them out algebraically (where $\times$ and y are two randomly selected numbers):

1. $(2x) + (2y) = 2\,(x + y) = 2$ times $(x + y) = $ **Even**

2. $(2x + 1) + (2y + 1) = [2x + 2y] + 2 = [2$ times $(x + y)] + 2 = $ **Even**

3. $(2x + 1) + (2y) = [2x + 2y] + 1 = [2$ times $(x + y)] + 1 = $ **Odd**

It should follow then that, given such algebraic logic, the probability of obtaining an odd sum, or P (odd sum) $= \frac{1}{3}$.

I admire someone with strength of conviction, especially when an argument can be reinforced by factual information. Unfortunately, the true test of mathematical accuracy rests with numbers themselves—*in vino veritas* (as the ancient Romans would say), or, for us, "the proof is in the pudding."

There is a distinct difference between the theoretical (idealism) and the empirical (realism). In this chapter, we will look at the power of numbers and how they can be used either to prove or to disprove popular assertions.

The process of stating-testing-adjusting is known by several names, most notably in the scientific community as the **scientific method**. A statistician would recognize the same process as hypothesis testing, but both scientific method (in middle school) and hypothesis testing (in high school) are usually introduced to students after they have left the elementary grades.

Younger students seem to be able to "play" with numbers more readily than their older counterparts and should be encouraged to do so wherever possible. This is just such an occasion: practicing arithmetic skills, generating data, and making predictions based on that data.

Just like with geometric figures, playing with numbers yields positive results. In short, we want to let students see what numbers can do for them, as opposed to what numbers have a tendency to do to them (in order to gain confidence, not lose it).

The Odd-Even chart (Figure 5.1) allows for answers to be recorded either as an "Odd" (**O**) answer or as an "Even" (**E**) answer.

#	O	E	#	O	E	#	O	E	#	O	E	#	O	E
1			11			21			31			41		
2			12			22			32			42		
3			13			23			33			43		
4			14			24			34			44		
5			15			25			35			45		
6			16			26			36			46		
7			17			27			37			47		
8			18			28			38			48		
9			19			29			39			49		
10			20			30			40			50		

Totals →   Odd: _____   out of 50 = _____ %

                   Even: _____   out of 50 = _____ %

Figure 5.1

Note: A blackline master of the chart can be found in the appendix. Also, if you are teaching the very youngest children (Grades K–1), you may want to skip the chart recording part altogether and concentrate solely on using the ODDOREVN program to reinforce addition skills (perhaps on the overhead).

CALCULATOR APPLICATION (GRADES K–4)

Determining the Sum of Two Randomly Selected Numbers as Odd or Even

The original program, ODDOREVN, is probably the most efficient way for a student to be exposed to a rapid series of two random natural numbers, self-quiz (flashcard style) for each of their sums, and tell whether those sums are odd or even (answers to be verbalized beforehand).

Students should be paired—one student answers the first 25 questions, the other checks answers on an Odd-Even chart (Figure 5.1)—and then switch roles:

```
PROGRAM:ODDOREVN
:ClrScreen
:Disp "THIS_PROGRAM"
:Disp "ADDS_2_RAN
DOM"
:Disp "NOS._BETWEEN"
:Disp "1_AND_10"
:Pause
:ClrScreen
:Disp "AND_TELLS_YOU"
:Disp "IF_THE_SUM_IS"
:Disp "_"
:DISP "'ODD' or 'EVEN'"
:Lbl 99
:randInt(1,10) -> A
:randInt(1,10) -> B
```

```
:Pause
:ClrScreen
:Disp "THE_SUM_OF
_,"A
:Disp "_and_,"B
:Disp "__="
:Pause
:Disp A+B
:Pause
:If fPart ((A+B)/ 2) =0
:Then
:Disp "_____EVEN"
:Else
:Disp "_____ODD"
:End
:Goto 99
```

Note: For the Erase Phase and for directions on how to either reset or escape the following, please refer to the MULTFRAX program in the introduction to Chapter 1: Numbers and Operations.

Input	**Output**

PRGM
Scroll down (Arrow Down) to ODDOREVN
ENTER

```
prgmODDOREVN
```

Note: Because of the random nature of how each calculator selects its numbers, the following contains examples of what you might see.

Input	**Output**
ENTER	THIS PROGRAM ADDS 2 RANDOM NOS. BETWEEN 1 AND 10
ENTER	AND TELLS YOU IF THE SUM IS 'ODD' OR 'EVEN'

ENTER
The student should say "5" before pushing . . .
ENTER
. . . and should say "ODD"
before pushing . . .
ENTER
	THE SUM OF
	          3
	and
	          2
	=
	          (5)
	          (ODD)

ENTER
The student should say "12" before pushing . . .
ENTER . . . and should say "EVEN"
before pushing . . .
ENTER
	THE SUM OF
	          8
	and
	          4
	=
	          (12)
	          (EVEN)

Note: The entries in parentheses in the last two output panels indicate that those answers do not appear until the **ENTER** button is pushed.

To disengage from the program, simply push 2nd **OFF, ON,** then **CLEAR.**

Figure 5.2 represents a filled-in sample of the chart. Interestingly, even though there were smaller stretches of Even results dominating Odd results (like from the 10th to the 20th answer), all 50 recorded results were split in half (25 Odd, 25 Even).

And herein lies the power of numbers to which I referred earlier. The more a particular experiment (process) is repeated, the closer one gets to the truth. Recall that the teacher whose class was observed stated that the probability of the sum of two randomly selected numbers is odd is $\frac{1}{3}$, but the data suggest that the probability of an odd result is actually closer to $\frac{25}{50}$ or $\frac{1}{2}$.

This phenomenon of actual (empirical/experimental) probability proving or disproving theoretical probability is called the **Law of Large Numbers**. This concept was also discussed in the previous *Key Concepts* volumes (McNamara, 2003, 2007).

So, we need to reevaluate our position (the third step in the aforementioned process of stating-testing-adjusting). A little backwards thinking might be helpful here, for doesn't $\frac{1}{2}$ also equal $\frac{2}{4}$? Could it be possible that, rather than the three cases stated at the beginning of this piece, there exist *four* scenarios by which an even and an odd number interact?

#	O	E	#	O	E	#	O	E	#	O	E	#	O	E
1	X		11	X		21	X		31		X	41	X	
2		X	12		X	22	X		32	X		42		X
3	X		13	X		23		X	33	X		43	X	
4	X		14		X	24	X		34		X	44	X	
5		X	15		X	25	X		35	X		45		X
6		X	16		X	26		X	36		X	46		X
7	X		17		X	27		X	37	X		47		X
8	X		18		X	28	X		38		X	48	X	
9	X		19	X		29		X	39	X		49		X
10			20		X	30		X	40	X		50	X	

Totals →   Odd: _____   out of 50 = _____%

Even: _____   out of 50 = _____%

Figure 5.2

Consider that the process of addition is one of four **binary operations** (along with subtraction, multiplication, division) we have—meaning that our minds take one number, select and apply an algorithmic process, and then bring in a second number.

Let's follow the addition of two numbers as a binary operation with the help of a **tree diagram** (Figure 5.3). The two lateral paths (Odd + Odd, Even + Even) lead to Even results. But, not one but two medial paths (Odd + Even, Even + Odd) lead to Odd results.

Each of the four paths is equally likely ($P = \frac{1}{4}$), since two of them are desired (the two Odds), P (an Odd result): $\frac{2}{4} = \frac{1}{2}$.

As a condensation of the previous diagram, a binary operation (+) system is constructed (Figure 5.4). The four results in the lower quadrant of the system— two of each being "Odd"—support the tree diagram in the affirmation that P (Odd sum) = $\frac{1}{2}$:

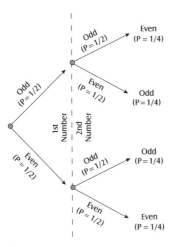

Figure 5.3

+	Odd	Even
Odd	Even	Odd
Even	Odd	Even

Figure 5.4

READ MORE ABOUT IT!

(Grades K–8) (Materials: A daily newspaper, pencil and paper, optional globe)

NCTM Standard: Formulate questions that can be addressed with data and collect, organize, and display relevant data in order to answer them.

One of the many elusive goals in today's classrooms is for teachers to improve students' reading skills—apparently without the help of J. K. Rowling and her fictional boy wizard.

Now, there certainly are students—though, I suspect, far fewer than are "diagnosed" as being the case (see the overprescription of Ritalin in the United States)—who labor in school with modest to severe learning disabilities. That being said, there are still more than a few other students who don't read well . . . simply because they *just don't read*!

Blame the malady on whatever you will—the breakdown of the American nuclear family, the pervasiveness of a media-induced culture, blah, blah. The

Chinese have a philosophy of addressing issues in a more head-on direction, though. They say, "Don't fix the blame. Fix the problem."

And the problem in this country impacts every subject educators teach, including my beloved mathematics. So, how can a teacher combine both reading and math into some interesting, up-to-date lessons for *all* students?

For my money (and I'll gladly shell out this pittance every time), no day is complete without reading a daily newspaper cover to cover. Politics aside (and a rational desire to see two points of view), there are math opportunities galore for even the youngest students—with the additional benefit of maybe, just maybe, turning some of them on to the joy of reading for fun.

Here are some examples of where to go within the pages of a newspaper to get math and work with a lot of numbers. Much of this information is usable for data analysis and statistical purposes:

How Many Sections Are There?

Starting with the letter "A" and seeing that the last section of the newspaper is section "E," how many sections are there altogether? Our daily local paper is generally divided into the following sections:

A—National and International News
B—Local News
C—Sports and Business
D—Living/Health/Food/Comics
E—Classified

Students should be able to see that Section A is first, Section B is second, and so on, up to five total sections (where E = the 5th letter).

Will There Be a "Sniglet" in This Section?

Because newspapers print on both sides of a piece of paper, the number of pages in any section will be even (recall how even numbers are defined as multiples of two). But some even numbers are more desirable than others—for certain types of readers, that is. It turns out that a piece of newspaper actually contains two pages of print on both its front and back, is folded, and is sequenced properly with the other pages in a section.

For example, suppose we had an eight-page tabloid (booklike) section. The front of Paper 1 would have page 8 and page 1 (reading left to right) so that, when the paper is folded back in its accustomed format, page 1 is first and page 8 is last. Turning Paper 1 over, we would find page 2 and page 7 (left to right). Inside, Paper 2 would have page 6 and page 3 (left to right) on the front and page 4 and page 5 (left to right) on the back.

Tabloid newspaper readers such as some commuters who open a section and crease it differently along the fold find sections with 6, 10, 14, 18, 22, 26, or 30 pages more clumsy than those with 8, 12, 16, 20, 24, 28, or 32 pages.

Why? Because that first subset of even-numbered pages would have to have that annoying two-sided "sniglet" piece of paper, which is hard to manage on windy days and sometimes gets misplaced altogether.

So, if the even number is *also* a multiple of 4 (the second subset), reading the paper is less of a struggle for those alternative reader-folders.

How Many Columns of Print Are on This Page?

It is interesting to compare newspapers as to how many columns of print there actually are. Who among us hasn't opened a box or can of something and noticed how much space there was inside? Some newspapers use the same cost-efficient methods: decrease the number of columns (from six to five in many cases) and/or widen the margins between columns (the wider-margin trick was used by many of my college classmates—I, for one, was appalled!).

Other tricks employed by newspapers include making the size of the print itself a point larger (perhaps by changing the font so as to be less obvious) or using smaller sheets of paper. Both, however, are difficult to detect.

What's the Color Ratio in This Section?

How many of the pictures in this section are in color? Have students pick any section of the newspaper (besides Classifieds) and count the number of pictures (both color and black-and-white). Then, have them count how many of those pictures are in color.

The ratio of the number of color pictures to the total number of pictures can be made into a fraction, and then a decimal, and then a percentage. Again, it's interesting to compare, in this case the "color ratio" from similar sections of different newspapers or even from one section to another of the *same* paper.

How Much News? How Many Ads?

Since any page from a newspaper is rectangular and advertisements, in turn, are also mostly rectangular, students can hone their measurement skills with metric rulers and papers and pencils (with their calculators held in abeyance for checking).

The standard size of a printed page is roughly 56 cm-by-32 cm, which comes out to be just short of 1,800 square centimeters. To find out how much of that page contains actual news stories, subtract the rounded sum of the areas of all the advertisements from the number 1,800 (and you will be amazed at how little of the page is actually devoted to news).

Can You Find This Place?

A recent study performed by an independent research organization found that more than half of American high school students questioned couldn't find countries in the news like Iraq or North Korea on a map. Troublesome, yes, but when over half of those same students can't find the great state of Nebraska either, then, as they say, "Houston, we have a problem."

(I know this one! Give me a hint. What country is the state of Houston in?)

Part of the fascination I got with reading about happenings in other places was looking on a map to find exactly *where* these places were. Think of one's knowledge of geography in the same context as spatial awareness, and that skill can be aided by extending coordinate geometry to **latitude** and **longitude**.

Starting with a globe and its grids clearly drawn, students should be able to locate the big horizontal middle line (like the x-axis) known as the **equator**. The equator is actually what is known as a **"great circle"** (a giant "hoop" with the longest diameter) and horizontally divides the globe into northern and southern hemispheres (the prefix "hemi-" standing for half of a sphere or ball).

(A great *Final Jeopardy* answer: "This world capital is closest to the equator." The question: "What is Quito?" (the logical response, of course, because Quito is the capital of Ecuador, the Spanish term for equator).

Sideways lines drawn parallel up from the equator (north) or down from the equator (south) are known as latitudes ("lat," the Latin term for "side" as we saw in "equilateral"). The equator is called 0° latitude, and latitudes count up to 90° north (the North Pole) and down to 90° south (the South Pole).

The "y-axis" counterpart to the equator is *not* as obvious to find. The great circle vertically passing through both poles is known as the **prime meridian** and passes through Greenwich, England, south of London, to establish GMT (Greenwich Mean Time), against which all the world's clocks are set.

Vertical lines drawn parallel left of the prime meridian (west) or right of the prime meridian (east) are known as longitudes. The prime meridian is called 0° longitude, and latitudes count up to 180° in both directions. Think about it—180° in one direction and 180° in the other equals 360° all the way around the world (where each degree is about 67 miles, making the length of the equator a little more than 24,000 miles long).

But, the two 180°'s have to meet somewhere on the other side of the globe, and they do—at the **International Date Line** in the middle of the Pacific Ocean (west of the Hawaiian Islands and east of New Zealand). Cross that line from east to west (heading by plane from, say, Los Angeles to Tokyo), and you have to move up one day in the calendar.

So, getting back to the prime meridian passing down through England, France, Spain, and western Africa, we call it 0° longitude. Now, move the class from a globe to a map, and, if the grid is properly drawn, everyone should be able to find where the two "axes" (the equator and the prime meridian) meet.

This "origin" of sorts (0° latitude and 0° longitude) meet quite inauspiciously at a point in the Gulf of Guinea, the body of water south of the capital city of Accra, Ghana, along Africa's Gold Coast. But, by doing so, they divide the entire map into four unofficial quarters, or **quadrants**: NW, SW, SE, and NE (reading counterclockwise from the upper left).

Therefore, if you want to find the relative position of a newspaper's dateline (the place which is cited at the top of an article), start your students' search at the "origin" on the map and have them read north/south first and west/east second for latitude and longitude, respectively.

(Cautionary note: Going up/down first and left/right second is *contrary* to how coordinates are read in coordinate geometry. Be careful here!)

Some examples: Iraq (34° north, 44° east); North Korea (39° north, 126° east); Nebraska (42° north, 100° west); Ecuador (1° south, 79° west); New Zealand (40° south, 176° east). Keep in mind also that Internet applications such as GoogleEarth.com will allow students to "zoom in" and verify their answers online—very cool!

It's also the case that a handful of cities—Washington, D.C., most prominent among them—actually label their thoroughfares with the "NW, SW, SE, or NE" suffix (the U.S. Capitol building acting as the "origin" for the city's grid pattern, as designed by the French engineer, Pierre L'Enfant). The official address for the White House, for example, is "1600 Pennsylvania Avenue, N.W."

Is It Hot Where You Are?

Who else in the United States will be as warm as we will be tomorrow? The weather page is one of several parts of a newspaper in which data abound. Students with the luxury of looking at a colorized map of the country should be able to start by finding their town and then noticing that their area shares a particular color (per a given temperature scale) with other parts of the country.

These **isotherms** (lines of equal temperature) are generally not as pronounced in the winter or summer months as they are in the more changeable spring and fall seasons. But this is not the only weather information that students may access from this page:

- Listings of projected high and low temps in cities around the country (leading to calculating the statistical measure of dispersion known as **range**, the difference between a high and a low).
- Question: Do the high temps of the U.S. cities listed visually match their positioning in the isotherm map of the country?
- Listings of projected high and low temps in cities around the world (Geography question: Where are Amsterdam, Beijing, Cairo, Dublin, etc., and what are their respective latitudes and longitudes?)
- Yesterday's 24-hour local temperatures (usually presented as a line graph, with warmer temperatures associated with daylight hours, etc.)
- Local sunrise and sunset times (Question: In hours and minutes, how much daylight might we expect to receive on a cloudless day?)
- Monthly and yearly totals of precipitation and their respective differentials (+ or −) and relative percentages

- Question: If the monthly precipitation in a cold-weather city's newspaper is listed as 1 inch of liquid, how much snow would actually have fallen?
- Environmental question: What are the effects of having too little or too much precipitation in a particular area over an extended length of time?

Did We Make Any Money in the Stock Market Yesterday?

Each member of a class of, say, twenty students brings an extra 50¢ with them to school one day for the purpose of getting into the stock market. There are online brokers (or, if you are fortunate to know one in your locale) who will invest $10.00 for you (20 students × $0.50 each) so that a class can follow the ups and downs of a share of stock in a chosen company (one that is listed in the paper as selling its shares at around $10.00 per share).

Of course, the Business section of the newspaper will contain that information, as well as its progress (make or lose money) from the previous day's market activity. A typical listing will contain data that include the high and low price of a share of stock over the past 52 weeks (another example of range).

But a second piece of information that will definitely generate more interest involves the last two columns—Last (price of the previous business day's trading session) and Change (±, "plus or minus," from the business day before last). Working backwards, the class should be able to figure out what the price of their share of stock was before the previous day's session began.

For example, if Last = $10.60 and Chg. (Change) = $0.24, that means that the share's price opened at $10.36 (which, reversing the process, is $10.60 − $0.24) and made 24¢ for the day by the time the market closed.

So, overall, since the class originally invested $10.00 and the price of the share is currently at $10.60, we could contact our broker (if we wanted to), sell our share back to the company, and receive 60¢ profit ($10.60 − $10.00). Taking that 60¢ and dividing it by 20, we would make each student investor 3¢ richer by having invested in the stock market!

Or, we could forgo contacting our broker and just keep an eye on the stock as it moves up and down all school year long. Lots of fun for everyone—a good, yet painless, learning experience in the risks (the ups and downs) of a certain type of investment—and another reason to read the newspaper every day!

Who's on First?

When I was growing up and visiting my maternal grandparents, I noticed that my grandpa always brought in his just-delivered copy of the (then) *Buffalo Evening News*, open it on the fold, and pull out the Sports section. When I once asked him why he did that before reading the rest of the paper, he answered, "Because I want to read about man's successes first before I read about his failures." (If he were still with us, wouldn't he be shocked to read a Sports section today!)

Combine that influence with a father whose outstanding merits athletically warranted induction into the Greater Buffalo Sports Hall of Fame, and you can see why I, as an only child, developed an intense passion for the games we play. Dad's accomplishments included serving for nearly forty years as president of a professional baseball league (the Class A New York–Pennsylvania League) and for a good portion of that time on the Professional Baseball Rules Committee.

So, with apologies to readers who either do not share my enthusiasm for athletics or have a love for some other sport, let me devote a little space to some of the statistics available in the Sports pages keyed to the great game of baseball. Follow Grandpa's lead, open that section, and you'll come upon a virtual mother lode of numbers each and every day between the months of March (spring training) and October (the playoffs and World Series).

The pennant races in the various professional leagues (six divisions in the major leagues alone) are always fun to follow—especially if you have a rooting interest for a particular team (my favorite resides in the capital of Massachusetts). Let's look at those standings, particularly the categories "Pct." (percentage of games played that have been won) and "G.B." (games behind).

To calculate the "Pct." listed for each team (the first tiebreaker in determining a division's final standings), divide the number of games any team has won by the total number of games it has played. So, if a team has played 10 games and won 6 of those games, its winning "Pct." would be $6 \div 10 = .600$.

It turns out that .600 is a significant percentage in the context of the Law of Large Numbers. Think about a winning percentage of .600: An amateur team playing only 10 games would be 6–4 (wins-losses), but a team in the major leagues playing a 162-game schedule would be 97–65 and in playoff contention. Just like before with the results of adding odd and even numbers, there is always strength in numbers.

Let's illustrate how to calculate entries in the "G.B." column with a quick example. Team A (30–18, pct. = .625) is ahead of Team B (25–22, pct. = .532) in the current standings. Take the difference in the two teams' wins ($30 - 25 = 5$) and the difference in their losses ($22 - 18 = 4$), add those two results ($5 + 4 = 9$), and divide that result by 2 ($9 \div 2 = 4.5$ games behind). So, G.B. equals the average of the sum of the differences of two teams' wins and losses.

As far as individual statistics go, it seems the sky's the limit. Probably the two that get the most scrutiny are batting average for a hitter and earned-run average for a pitcher. Both calculations use formulas, of course, but they can also make a lot of sense if you think about them.

Batting average (the listing "Avg." in a box score) is simply the number of hits a batter collects divided by the number of at-bats. (There are various exceptions to what's counted as a hit or an at-bat but, for the purpose of the compilation, let's keep things basic.)

Suppose a batter flies out in one at-bat but also hits a double and a single in his other two at-bats. So, two hits are divided by three at-bats: $2 \div 3 = .667$. Wow! This batter had a good game hitting that day, which is once again problematic under the tyranny of the Law of Larger Numbers.

Batting average is an accumulated measure of success. In the major league ranks, out of the 400 of so "everyday" players (those who don't pitch), only a small percentage (less than 10%) have batting averages higher than .300, meaning that the vast majority hit in the .200's. The major leaguer who has one good game hitting .667, can also "look forward" to many more bad games not getting a hit at all because his average is computed over 162 games.

For baseball followers who study the numbers on pitchers, earned-run average can have an almost-mysterious quality to it—if only because the clarity of an "earned" run (much like the infield fly rule) has tested the greatest legal scholars of our time. Nonetheless, again with the benefit of an example, let's suppose a pitcher allows two earned runs in three innings (one-third of a nine-inning complete game) before being replaced.

Had this pitcher pitched the entire nine-inning game (three times as long) at that rate, he or she would have allowed $2 \times 3 = 6$ earned runs, which is a one-game "ERA" of 6.00. Its formula brings the process into sharper focus:

$$\text{ERA} = (\text{number of earned runs} \div \text{number of innings pitched}) \times 9$$

Over the course of the season, it is hoped this pitcher gets his ERA down to more respectable level: under 4.00 is fair, under 3.50 is good, under 3.00 is excellent. The Law of Large Numbers will work to a positive advantage here if this pitcher can last longer and do a better job getting the other team to make outs.

Other sports generate excellent numbers of their own. But baseball is truly a statistician's paradise—and the greatest show on dirt.

What's on TV?

Surprisingly, the relatively new matrix format of newspaper television listings has more than its fair share of inherent math. In the interest of saving valuable space, newspapers have eschewed the traditional column-type list of programs in favor of a large rectangle with times across the top and outlets along the side (sometimes grouped by networks, basic cable, premium cable, and so forth). A horizontal read lists all the programs being shown by a particular outlet, and a vertical read allows a viewer to see what programming choices are available at a particular time.

The math to which I referred is nothing less than comparisons and additions (several with fractions). And some newspapers will do those interested a favor by literally using 30-minute squares as their basic unit of measure.

Let's consider prime-time programming (shows that air during a three-hour block of weeknight time). During a specific hour, one network might air two 30-minute comedies while another network (listed right below it) might air an hourlong medical drama. Depending on your class, this relationship might be described as $30 + 30 = 60$, or $\frac{1}{2} + \frac{1}{2} = 1$, or a ratio of areas = 1:2.

A two-hour movie might be airing on one network while a second network listed immediately below it might program the same two hours with two half-hour comedies and an hourlong crime drama: $30 + 30 + 60 = 120$, or $\frac{1}{4} + \frac{1}{4} + \frac{1}{2} = 1$, or the areas ratio of the comedy to the movie = 1:4.

Where Are the Comics?

Those of us who are regular newspaper readers have our favorite comic strips, but let me alert you to the creative geometries created by the incredible minds of cartoonists.

Get a (color) copy of the Sunday comics, and do a little careful research:

- How many strips are simply composed of standard framed squares (with each panel the same size)?
- How many contain an occasional unframed square?
- How many contain a combination of squares and rectangles?
- Are there any strips with other types of frames (e.g., circles)?
- Do any strips have imbedded or overlapping frames?

The colors, the shapes, the dialogue, the story, the punch line—they're all found in the comics.

What's a Six-Letter Word for Logic?

For me, and to borrow the tag line from the old orange juice TV ads, a morning without a puzzle is like a day without sunshine. I used to look forward to my daily crossword puzzle (more about that in a moment), but I have been swept away by Sudoku.

The Sudoku puzzle consists of filling in a partially completed 9-by-9 grid so that every row, every column, and each of the nine subset 3-by-3 boxes has the numbers 1 through 9 with no repeats allowed. The puzzles come in various degrees of difficulty, but there is no math involved, just creative thinking. This is a wonderful activity for children and adults alike and can be done in hardcopy form or online.

The daily newspaper crossword puzzle (see the movie documentary, *Wordplay*) in some respects is to Sudoku what chess is to checkers. The completion of a crossword puzzle requires retention of words and knowledge in direct proportion to the puzzle's level of difficulty, so not as large a percentage of students will persevere.

However, every student should be able to recognize and appreciate how every brand-new crossword puzzle grid has point rotation symmetry. Students can eyeball the center tile (black or white), place the point of their pencils on that tile, and half-turn the paper so as to create the exact same grid pattern.

Want to Catch a Movie Tonight?

A simple form of review to which all of us can relate is the 4-star rating system (or slight variation thereof) that most newspaper movie critics use.

Using 4 stars (out of 4) as that reviewer's mark of critical acclaim (an outstanding work), the general scaling gives 3.5 stars for excellent, 3 for very good, 2.5 for good, 2 for satisfactory, 1.5 for fair-to-poor, 1 for poor, 0.5 for very poor, and no stars for don't bother wasting your hard-earned money. However, for the quick skim-through read, the stars actually appear somewhere in the review: * * * * = Outstanding   * * * = Very Good   * * = Satisfactory   * = Poor.

This use of pictorial symbols to represent words, ideas, or sounds (e.g., sheet music) is known as a **pictograph** and traces its roots back to the hieroglyphics drawn by the ancient Egyptians. There are, of course, more elaborate pictographs that are commonly printed in newspapers every day—e.g., six stalks of corn lined up next to each other (each stalk representing 1 million tons) to represent six million tons converted to ethanol in the United States last year.

For the true pictograph aficionado, there is no better daily presentation of pictographs (and other types of graphs) than those offered in the Snapshots collection printed in the well-known, high-color, nationally distributed weekday newspaper whose headquarters is in Fairfax, VA.

Remember: If you as teacher want students to be better readers, you have to present all kinds of stimuli (13 were listed above, but there most certainly are more for you to consider.) Invite them to join you in the excitement and the possibilities of the newspaper, for your encouragement might provide the spark of natural curiosity for a younger child to want to read more about it.

LIVING GRAPHS

(Grades K–6) (Materials: Interlocking colored cubes, 3 worksheets, pencil, optional compass)

NCTM Standard: Select and use appropriate statistical methods so as to analyze data.

A teacher who opens a textbook and uses preconceived sets of data to teach is really missing a great opportunity for class engagement—especially when instructing our youngest students. A good analogy would be the difference between store-bought food and food made from scratch—no doubt the former saves time, but the latter always tastes fresher and better and, thus, is worth the extra time (the difference between eating and dining).

As a bonus for your extra effort, you'll soon discover that not only do younger students get into generating their own data but they also enjoy being part of the resulting graphs—known as "living graphs." Below are three basic—yet fun—examples of how students can play a central role in the success of a data gathering/graphing lesson:

Gender Differences

A typical instructional approach might go something like this: "Using the circle graph (Figure 5.5), determine the number of girls and the number of boys in a class of 20 students."

So, the students take out their notebooks and listen to their teacher set up the percent problem: "What is 40% of 20?" . . . and so on and so forth.

A more engaging approach might be to have your own class of 20 lie in a circle in the middle of the room (feet toward the center) with girls in one sector and boys in the other (Figure 5.6). Try to get equal spacing of students in both sectors. Place strips of tape on the floor to separate the sectors (radii). To make the circle, have students hold a long piece of string over their heads and tie the ends together.

The teacher then stands up on a nearby desk or stepstool and snaps a picture with a digital or a Polaroid camera. Students return to their desks and get to glimpse (as the teacher moves about the room) the living graph of which each was a part. Have the students try to recreate the picture as a drawn circle graph (maybe on paper with the circle already in place).

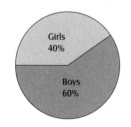

Figure 5.5

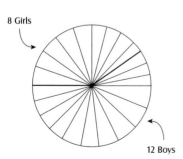

8 Girls

12 Boys

Figure 5.6

Then, and only then, does the relevant arithmetic come into play:

How many girls? (8) How many boys? (12) How many students altogether? (8 + 12 = 20) How could we check our answer? (One student gets to go about the room and gently touch everyone on the shoulder while the class counts aloud.)

What is the ratio of girls to the entire class? (8:20) How may we make that into a fraction? $(8:20 = \frac{8}{20})$ Reduced? $(\frac{8}{20} = \frac{4}{10} = \frac{2}{5})$ Into a decimal? $(\frac{4}{10} = .40)$ Into a percent? $(.40 = 40\%)$

How about the boys? Ratio? (12:20) Fraction? $(12:20 = \frac{12}{20})$ Reduced? $(\frac{12}{20} = \frac{6}{10} = \frac{3}{5})$ Percent? $(\frac{6}{10} = 60\%)$

Check our percent answers? $(40\% + 60\% = 100\% \ldots$ Yes, it checks!)

See the difference? Much, *much*, more inclusive, challenging, and interesting.

Favorite Colors

Again, assuming that you have 20 students in your room, pair them off and give each partnership a large rectangular piece of plain cardboard (perhaps 6 inches in width by 3 feet in length). Each pair of students will then use the appropriate tool (marker/crayon/paint) to work together and color their cardboard with one of the following ten assigned colors: **white, pink, red, brown, orange, yellow, light green, dark green, light blue,** or **black**.

Recall the large source/container of cubes used in previous chapters. Each student individually—and in an orderly fashion—gets to pick one cube from the central container representing her or his favorite color (it does not have to be the same color as that just used to color the cardboard).

The teacher then clears the middle of the classroom and places the colored cardboard in a row (called a **spectrogram**) in the order indicated above. Each student is then asked to leave his or her chair with favorite color cube in hand and form an orderly line behind whichever color along the cardboard spectrogram is preferred—another "living graph."

The teacher may again use either a digital camera or a Polaroid from a moderate height in order to make a visual record of the class's favorite colors (a **bar graph**). As before, the picture should be saved so that it may shared later.

Alternative step (if necessary): Students then place their favorite color cube on the spot where they are standing before returning to their seats. In effect, the class has created a new bar graph representing their preferences.

At this point, one student from each partnership goes to the cubes container, takes ten cubes (one of each color), and returns to her or his partner. Using the "floor model" cardboard spectrogram still in place, partners should quickly be able to snap their ten cubes together in the order suggested to form a smaller scale spectrogram (as illustrated in Figure 5.7):

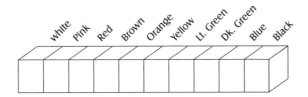

Figure 5.7

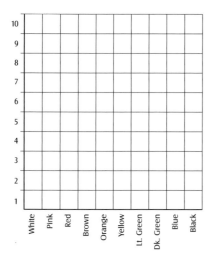

Figure 5.8

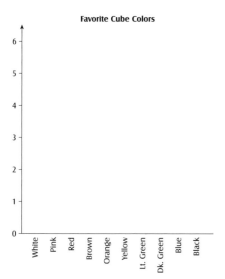

Figure 5.9

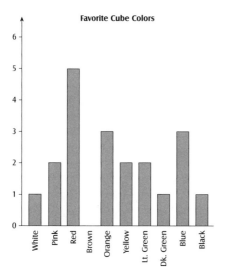

Figure 5.10

The teacher then passes out to each partnership copies of a tally grid (Figure 5.8), each box being at least 3 cm-by-3 cm. (A blackline master appears in the appendix.) Students are asked to count aloud (in order, left to right) the number of cubes that comprise each of the color categories on the floor-model bar graph (or digital picture, if preferred). Those ten "counts" are written along the bottom of the tally grid under each color.

One student from each partnership now goes back to the cube container and retrieves the same number of cubes of each color indicated on the tally grid. Starting along the bottom, the cubes are then placed in vertical grid boxes going up and above each color word on the sheet.

Note: It is important at this point to emphasize that the bars of a bar graph never touch each other ("Bar None"). That's why the boxes in the tally grid should be drawn at least 3 cm-by-3 cm in order to accommodate the cubes (which are each 2 cm-by-2 cm).

The teacher then passes out rulers and copies of the new sheet entitled "Favorite Cube Colors" (Figure 5.9; see the blackline master in the appendix). On the blackboard or overhead, the teacher demonstrates to the class how to draw rectangles that represent the bars of a bona fide bar graph. (Students might want to snap cubes together of the same color to help them with the heights of the bars.)

Let's assume our class of twenty students had the following preferences: White = 1, Pink = 2, Red = 5, Brown = 0, Orange = 3, Yellow = 2, Light Green = 2, Dark Green = 1, (Light) Blue = 3, and Black = 1. Those numbers serve as the heights of each of the respective bars comprising the completed bar graph (Figure 5.10). Both the floor model and the tally grid serve as transitional pieces for the teacher and every student interested in an accurate finished product.

The mean as a line of reflection: For older students who might appreciate something visual and a little bit out of the ordinary, let's continue by computing the mean number of cubes in each color category: number of students ÷ number of colors = 20 ÷ 10 = a mean (average) of 2 cubes for each color.

So, on the just-completed bar graph, use the ruler and draw a horizontal line through the "2" along the vertical axis (Figure 5.11). As the reader can see, there are three vertical bars extending above that line.

Those three pieces may now be "broken off" and used as fillers below the horizontal mean line 2. As represented in Figure 5.12, the piece above Blue is used to bring Black up to 2; the piece above Orange is used to do a similar service for Dark Green; and the piece above Red is subdivided into two pieces to help both White and Brown get up to 2.

One final instructional note: The focus of the "spectro-bar graph" lesson was whole-group, followed by cooperative learning (pairing), and concluding with individual seatwork. The common thread was hands-on, but the design was reversed and intentionally engaging so as to involve every student immediately. And, should the teacher feel confident, a visual application of transformational geometry can help students gain a fuller understanding of the meaning of mean.

Falling Leaves

Whether they be gathered during a playground scavenger hunt or perhaps brought to school protected by wax paper, the leaves of autumn offer beauty, variety, and live-science learning possibilities.

Pique the interest of even your most skeptical students by beginning this lesson with a Google search of leaves on the Internet. Look for information that addresses such issues as photosynthesis (the lack of chlorophyll as the reason why leaves change color) and for leaves from various types of trees (evergreen needles, for example, actually qualify as leaves).

Many of the steps taken after each student has chosen a favorite leaf are the same as in the previous lesson with colored cubes. But there are significant differences as well, "stemming" (bad pun) from the tiny canal system (known as **veins**) running through most leaves that is visible to the naked eye.

This time, the teacher sticks two strips of electric tape on the classroom floor, creating an "L-shaped" pair of intersecting axes at a common origin. Then on two pieces of paper or cardboard the teacher writes the words "Number of Veins" and "Number of Leaves" and places them along the horizontal and vertical axes, respectively.

The students then examine their leaves and count the number of veins (including the big vertical middle vein resembling a river in the middle of the leaf). Afterward, in an orderly fashion, each student goes to the "living graph" on the floor and places his or her leaf in the appropriate column (as in Figure 5.13).

Note: The arrows at the end of each axis (and the absence of numbers along the vertical axis) are to accommodate more leaves and/or more veins.

This new "floor model" will eventually be made into a **histogram**, which, even though it will have bars of its own, is not considered to be a bar graph. The horizontal axis of a bar graph involves categories (qualitative), while that of a histogram involves numbers (quantitative). And, while the bars of a bar graph don't touch ("Bar None"), those of a histogram do.

(See the "TOG" in the middle of the word "hisTOGram?" Think of the first three letters of the word "TOGETHER," and you'll remember that a histogram's bars touch!)

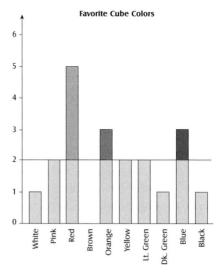

Figure 5.11

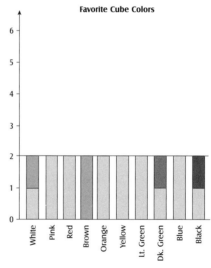

Figure 5.12

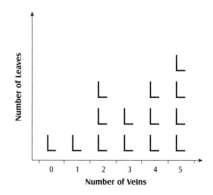

Figure 5.13

The teacher then supplies each student with a ruler and a precopied "L-shaped" set of axes (Figure 5.14). (See the appendix for a blackline master.) Just like before, students examine the final version of the graph on the floor and/or a posting of the final tally for each number of veins supplied by the teacher on the blackboard or overhead.

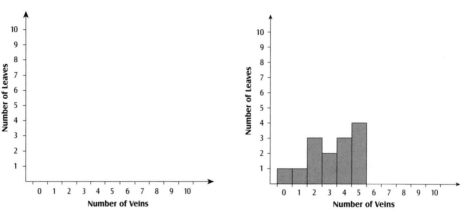

Figure 5.14   **Figure 5.15**

Then, with the teacher helping to get the class started, each student eventually fills in the paper with touching bars (Figure 5.15). For this example, one should be able to see that, in our class of 20 students, 1 leaf had 0 veins, 1 leaf had 1 vein, 3 leaves had 2 veins, 2 leaves had 3 veins, and so on.

FIRE AND ICE

(Grades 3–8) (Materials: Listed below)

NCTM Standard: Develop and evaluate inferences and predictions that are based on data.

It's mid-January, and life in a Northern town can be a bit of a struggle. The excitement of the holidays has come and gone, and you are running a little short of energy and fresh ideas. And, baby, it's cold and icy outside!

This is exactly the best time of the school year to try this unit with your students. Many participatory phases are part of this exercise: prediction, observation, graphing, and analysis. It combines math and science—and, the more theatric your presentation, the more suspense will build for your class.

Materials for the teacher:

One electric hot plate (at least 12" across)
One thermoplate cover (protects inquisitive fingers at all times)
One pair of rubberized scissor-clamps
Two oven gloves
Two one-liter laboratory beakers (preferably with unbreakable glass)
Two 12"-long Celsius (lab) thermometers
A ready supply of snow from outside (ice cubes work also, but not as well)
Tap water
Sink (for placing hot beakers afterwards)

Overhead "Time-Temp" graph paper
Two overhead markers: one red, one blue
Ruler

Materials for each student:

One piece of "Time-Temp" graph paper
    (blackline master in appendix)
Two markers: one red, one blue
Ruler

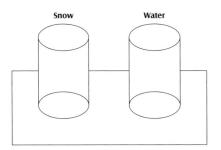

Figure 5.16

CAUTION: This activity requires utmost care . . . and room! Do NOT allow your students to get close, as there are many hot items within reach!

Recommended: A teacher aide for assistance and "crowd control."

Make sure students have all materials and do a quick inventory for yourself to make sure you have access to all of yours as well (especially the overhead, which will, ideally, be manned by the aide).

When everyone is set to begin, turn the hot plate on (allow time for full-power heating), and have the teacher aide fill one of the two beakers with tap water, the other with snow. Place one thermometer into each beaker. Before you set the beakers on the hot plate, ask the class to make a prediction (always a great way to involve everyone): "Which beaker do you think will boil first, the snow or the water?"

Most students will predict that the beaker filled with water will boil first—after all, a liquid should be able to boil faster than a frozen solid (which has to become a liquid before it can boil, right?). Hopefully, there will be one or two of your students who will predict otherwise, that the snow will boil first, and those students will take a bit of a razzing for doing so. (That's ok!)

Now that some time has elapsed, take a reading from both thermometers. Direct the aide and all of your students to put a red dot at 20°C, or room temperature, right along the temperature axis (red for liquid) and a blue dot at 0°C, or the origin (blue for frozen solid).

Please warn your students one more time before starting the demonstration!

The teacher then places the two beakers on the fully-heated hot plate at the very instant a visible clock's second hand is at "12." The two thermometers are then read for beaker temperatures every minute.

Have a blank piece of "Time-Temp" graph paper (Figure 5.17) ready. Every minute, you can stoke the momentum of the class by asking the students to watch the two beakers (changes will occur). Then, at minute intervals, take the two readings, saying things like, "I don't know. Something's happening here . . ."

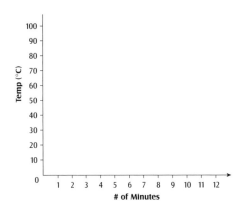

Figure 5.17

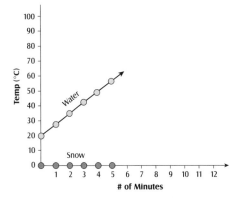

Figure 5.18

During the first five minutes (Figure 5.18), it appears that the beaker with the water is heating up at a fairly constant rate (represented mathematically by a straight line of red dots, or, here, empty circles).

Meanwhile, the beaker with the snow is still stuck at 0°C (blue dots, or, here, filled-in circles). But, the snow has melted considerably—so much so that only about 100 mL remain in the bottom of the beaker!

At about the 6-minute point and with the snow completely vanished (Figure 5.19), the remaining water in the original "snow" beaker begins to warm very rapidly (blue dots/filled-in circles on the graph). The all-water beaker, however, continues to warm at its constant rate (red dots/empty circles).

Looking at the two line graphs, it is around the 8-minute mark that the two lines intersect (Figure 5.20). Of course, what that means in the demonstration itself is that the two thermometers read about the same temperature.

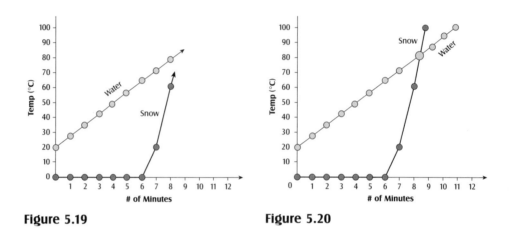

Figure 5.19   **Figure 5.20**

Now the questions for the class are: "Does anyone want to change their minds? Which beaker do you think is going to have its water boiling sooner now? Does anyone care to apologize to _____ for their earlier prediction?" And, it is not long after that the "snow" beaker's water begins to boil first (reaches 100°C).

CAUTION: The hot plate, and all materials that are hot (beakers, clamps), should now be well out of the way of your students. The hot plate especially should be insulated with a thermoplate cover that provides additional protection from burning accidents.

From an earth science standpoint, the snow actually demonstrated each of the three different types of matter. Because heat acted as an exciter of its molecules, the snow (solid) melted into water (liquid) and eventually, if left to boil until it is all evaporated, will turn into steam (gas).

Three other points can also be developed in this final analysis:

The first is that 1 liter (1,000 mL) of snow actually turned into 0.1 liter (100 mL) of water. There's a lot of air in water (which fish with gills have the means to access but humans don't), and one can see evidence of that air in the tiny bubbles that rise from the bottom of a pan of boiling water when heated on a stove.

The second point is the ratio itself that was just mentioned. If 1 liter of snow melts down to 0.1 liter of water (a 10:1 ratio), then, for every 10 inches of snow (the fluffy, mid-January type), there's an equivalent of 1 inch of water.

That's the reason why my part of the country (upstate New York) is so green in the spring and summer and so colorful in the fall—lots of water all year long, whether rain or snow (and all the snow we get in winter eventually melts).

One more point to observe is a very short (and somewhat rule-of-thumb) formula for finding out how long it takes snow to melt on a hot plate. Of course, there are two variables we observed: How much water? and What is the temperature of the water in the beaker when the beaker was put on the hot plate?

The formula my classes have used for determining how long it takes snow to melt on a hot plate is:

t = .14 × (amount of water in liters) × (100 − initial temperature).

Consider the 1 liter beaker of room-temperature tap water we just heated:

t = .14 × (1 L) × (100 − 20) = about 11.2 minutes

Now consider the .1 liter of snow (the formula didn't take effect until the snow turned to 0°C water):

t = .14 × (.1 L) × (100 − 0) = about 1.4 minutes (which then would be added to the six minutes or so for the snow-to-water conversion, making about 8 minutes or so for 1 liter of snow to "boil").

GAMES OF CHANCE

(Grades K–8) (Materials: Listed at the end of each activity)

NCTM Standard: Understand and apply basic concepts of probability.

Sports and recreational activities provide a ready-made and interesting backdrop for the study of a variety of probabilities. The next few pages present three situations for consideration, but clearly these could be amended or increased depending upon your and your students' common interests.

Velcro Ball Toss

Affix the circular velcro target on a classroom wall, and, like archery (but obviously not as dangerous), students can score points by tossing velcro balls that stick on the target (Figure 5.21).

Students of all ages can enjoy this activity, and certainly there are lots of whole-number addition (and even subtraction) scenarios that can emerge here. However, let's explore this question: "Are the point values listed on the target itself accurate (in other words, do they match the probabilities of success)?"

Let's first think of the target as a set of four concentric circles. There is one clear circle (the bull's eye) and three rings of increasing sizes emanating from the center. If the bull's eye has a diameter of 12" (Figure 5.22), its radius = 6" and its area = $\pi r^2 = \pi(6)^2 = 36\pi$.

The "5" ring (immediately around the bull's eye) is actually a circle of diameter 24" (Figure 5.23) but, like a doughnut, has its center (the bull's eye of area = 36?) taken away. Since its radius = 12", the "5" ring's area = $\pi(12)^2 - 36\pi = 144\pi - 36\pi = 108\pi$.

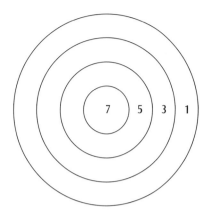

Figure 5.21   **Figure 5.22**

The "3" ring (immediately around the "5" ring) is actually a circle of diameter 36" (Figure 5.24) but, like a doughnut, has its center (the complete "5" circle of area = 144π) taken away. Since its radius = 18", the "3" ring's area = $\pi(18)^2 - 144\pi = 324\pi - 144? = 180\pi$.

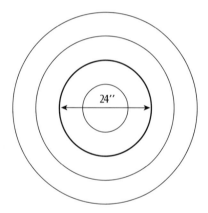

Figure 5.23   **Figure 5.24**

Finally, the "1" ring (immediately around the "3" ring) is actually a circle of diameter 48" (Figure 5.25) but, like a doughnut, has its center (the complete "3" circle of area = 324π) taken away. Since its radius = 24", the "1" ring's area = $\pi(24)^2 - 324\pi = 576\pi - 324\pi = 252\pi$.

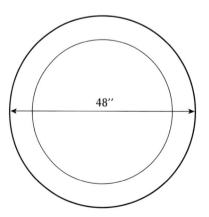

Figure 5.25

Putting all the pieces together, then, it turns out that the area of the bull's eye plus the areas of the three rings must equal 576π (the complete "1" circle). Now find (and reduce) the fractional parts of each of the four component parts (the bull's eye and the three rings):

Bull's Eye = $36\pi/576\pi = \frac{1}{16}$ of the entire target

"5" Ring = $108\pi/576\pi = \frac{3}{16}$ of the entire target

"3" Ring = $180\pi/576\pi = \frac{5}{16}$ of the entire target

"1" Ring = $252\pi/576\pi = \frac{7}{16}$ of the entire target

(Note: One may also get the same four fractions above by turning on the TI-73, dividing each fraction one at a time, and pressing the **F↔D** button.)

But notice the numerators of each fraction! Because hitting the bull's eye is the ultimate goal for any player, the numbers are reversed (7–5–3–1) to take into account the degree of difficulty for any one toss.

So, the answer is: Yes! The point values are indeed accurate!

Class Activity Options (answers tallied by a student of choice)

1. Velcro Ball Toss

2. Tennis Ball Toss (placing a target on the floor of the room)

3. Skee Ball (local carnival fundraisers may have access)

4. Archery (in gym class, the highest degree of care to be taken and only with the direct supervision of the Phys. Ed. Dept.!)

Penalty Kicks

When the men's teams from Italy and France met in the finals of the most recent World Cup (a soccer tournament held every four years to determine the finest team on the entire planet), the two evenly matched teams played to a 1–1 draw in regulation time followed by two scoreless overtimes.

The game—and the world championship—was then settled by penalty kicks.

For the uninformed, a penalty kick in soccer is basically a 12-yard shot taken by someone who can run as far and as fast as needed and fired at a rectangular goal 8 feet high and 24 feet across (Figure 5.26). A goalkeeper who cannot move until the ball is launched, sometimes at speeds exceeding 100 miles per hour, guards the goal. Wow!

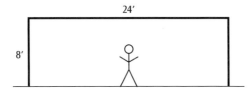

Figure 5.26

A probability question to consider is this: "What is the probability that a goalkeeper at any level of competition (never mind the immense talent displayed by world-class soccer players in the World Cup) ever does make a save?"

Answer: About 1 in 5 = .20 = 20% success.

Therefore, from the shooter's standpoint, his or her rate of success is the same as the goaltender's rate of failure; that is, if the goaltender fails 80% of the time, the shooter thus succeeds 80% of the time ($80\% = .80 = \frac{8}{10} = \frac{4}{5}$).

Class Activity Options (answers tallied by a student of choice)

1. Penalty kicks (12 yds. away) with a kick ball and a goalie

2. Kicks with a kick ball and no goalie from 6 yds., 12 yds., and 18 yds.

3. Throwing a ball or a Frisbee (with the same rules as 2 above)

4. Using a smaller (hockey) goal, outside or inside

Basketball: Three Ways to Score

When the basketball powers-that-be of the NCAA (National Collegiate Athletic Association) instituted a three-point arc 19 feet, 9 inches away from each basket in the mid-1990s, scholastic and youth leagues around the country adopted the same scoring arc distance for their participants (Figure 5.27).

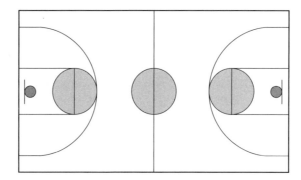

Figure 5.27

The dilemma for many coaches—especially those who coached in the days before the arc was instituted—is this: "Should I encourage my players to shoot lots of higher-risk three-point shots (beyond the arc), or should I stress that they be taking lower-risk two-point shots (inside the arc)?" This is actually a probability question in disguise.

A little research of the NCAA Web site (www.ncaa.org) reveals lots of data in many sports and different divisions, but, for our purposes, let's focus on some of the team statistics of the 2005–2006 Division I Men's Basketball season (of which there are 326 schools). By percentage, the best two-point shooting team was Texas A&M–Corpus Christi at just over 50%, and the best three-point shooting team was Southern Utah at just under 43%.

However, it would be a more representative measure to take the **median** percentage (the average of the teams at positions 163 and 164) for both categories—44% for two-pointers and 35% for three-pointers. Converting those two numbers to fractions (and rounding the 44% figure up just slightly to 45%), the two rounded results would be $\frac{9}{20}$ and $\frac{7}{20}$, respectively.

And, to complete the theoretical probabilities, the average success rate for team foul shooting (worth one point) is approximately $70\% = \frac{7}{10} = \frac{14}{20}$. So, given a class of 20 students, these tallies represent the number of shots that must be made for the class to meet the average success rate of top-level college teams:

Foul shots (one-pointers) = 14
Inside-the-arc field goals (two-pointers) = 9
Outside-the-arc field goals (three-pointers) = 7

Just like the World Cup soccer players, the athletes playing Division I NCAA Men's Basketball are pretty good, too!

Class Activity Options (answers tallied by a student of choice)

1. Basketball shooting in the gym: Different size balls must go into the basket and then they must hit the rim

2. Nerf ball shooting in class with different distances premarked

3. Paper wad tossing into a trash can in class (again, different distances premarked)

> Conclusion for Velcro Ball Toss, Penalty Kicks, and Basketball Shooting: The farther the distance from the target, the lower the probability of your success!

Appendix

Worksheet Blackline Masters

Notes

    1. Some worksheets may require size and/or image adjustments when copied.

    2. The following worksheets are framed/highlighted throughout the book—headings match with page numbers.

CHAPTER 1: DOUBLE TAKE

Name _____

Date _____

Student A _____ *Student B* _____				
	1st Picks A	1st Picks B	2nd Picks A	2nd Picks B
Card #1:				
Card #2:				
Sum:				
Difference:				
Product:				
Improper Fraction:				
Fraction Reduced:				
Mixed Number:				
Proper Fraction:				
Fraction Reduced:				
Decimal:				
Percent:				

CHAPTER 1: SIEVE OF ERATOSTHENES

Name _____

Date _____

1	2	3	4	5	6	7	8	9	10
11	12	13	14	15	16	17	18	19	20
21	22	23	24	25	26	27	28	29	30
31	32	33	34	35	36	37	38	39	40
41	42	43	44	45	46	47	48	49	50

CHAPTER 2: GROWING PATTERNS

Name _____

Date _____

Stair Steps	# Squares	How I Found It
1st		
2nd		
3rd		
4th		
5th		

CHAPTER 2: SQUARE SQUARES

Name _____

Date _____

Square Squares	# Squares	How I Found It
1st		
2nd		
3rd		
4th		
5th		

CHAPTER 2: CROSS NUMBERS

Name _____

Date _____

Cross Numbers	# Squares	How I Found It
1st		
2nd		
3rd		
4th		
5th		

CHAPTER 3: INTRODUCTION TO GEOMETRY

Name _____

Date _____

CHAPTER 3: GUESS MY PATTERN

Name _____

Date _____

	A	B	C	D
1				
2				
3				
4				

CHAPTER 3: CRAZY QUILTS

Name _____

Date _____

	A	B	C	D	E	F	G	H
8								
7								
6								
5								
4								
3								
2								
1								

CHAPTER 3: FOLD IT RIGHT THERE!

Name _____

Date _____

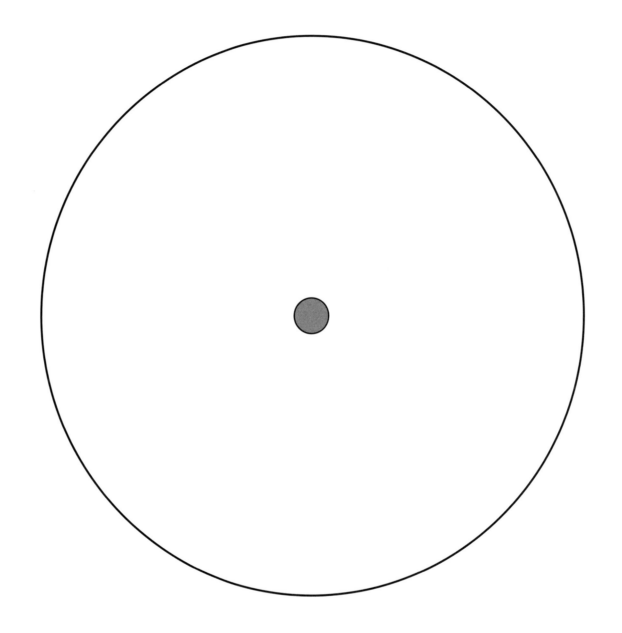

CHAPTER 4: I SCREAM . . . YOU SCREAM . . .

Name _____

Date _____

Name : _____

Quality Control Report

Shift (Period): _____

Ingredient	Amount Needed	Measuring Utensil Used	Amount Used (Show Calculations)
Example: Chocolate Syrup	$\frac{3}{4}$ teaspoon	$\frac{1}{4}$ teaspoon	$\frac{3}{4} \div \frac{1}{4} = \frac{3}{4} \times \frac{1}{4}$ = Three $\frac{1}{4}$ teaspoons
Ice			
Salt			
Half 'n Half			
Sugar			
Vanilla			

Signature of Department Manager (Teacher): _____

Comments From Your Taste-Testing: _____

_____

_____

_____

_____

CHAPTER 4: HOW THEY STACK UP

Worksheet 1

Name _____

Date _____

L	W	Perimeter (Add Edges)	Area (Add Faces)

CHAPTER 4: HOW THEY STACK UP

Worksheet 2

Name _____

Date _____

L	*W*	*H*	*Volume (Add Cubes)*	*Surface Area (Add Faces)*

CHAPTER 5: INTRODUCTION TO DATA ANALYSIS

Name _____

Date _____

#	O	E	#	O	E	#	O	E	#	O	E	#	O	E
1			11			21			31			41		
2			12			22			32			42		
3			13			23			33			43		
4			14			24			34			44		
5			15			25			35			45		
6			16			26			36			46		
7			17			27			37			47		
8			18			28			38			48		
9			19			29			39			49		
10			20			30			40			50		

Totals →   Odd: _____ out of 50 = _____%

Even: _____ out of 50 = _____%

CHAPTER 5: LIVING GRAPHS

Worksheet 1

Name _____

Date _____

	White	Pink	Red	Brown	Orange	Yellow	Lt. Green	Dk. Green	Blue	Black
10										
9										
8										
7										
6										
5										
4										
3										
2										
1										

CHAPTER 5: LIVING GRAPHS

Worksheet 2

Name _____

Date _____

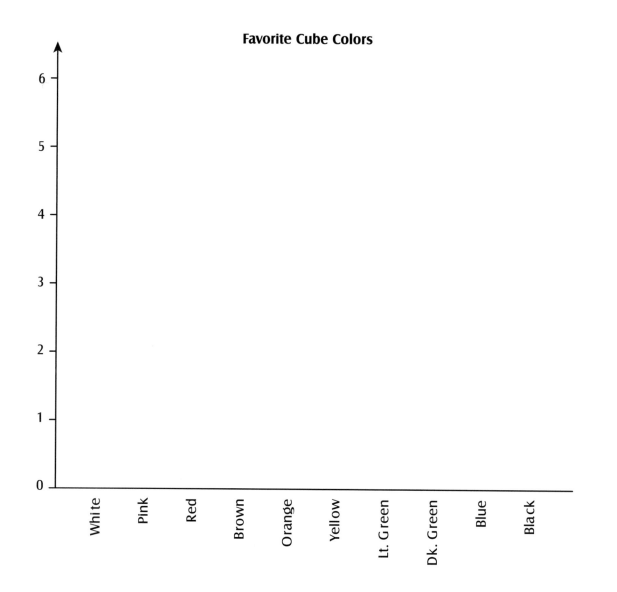

Favorite Cube Colors

CHAPTER 5: LIVING GRAPHS

Worksheet 3

Name _____

Date _____

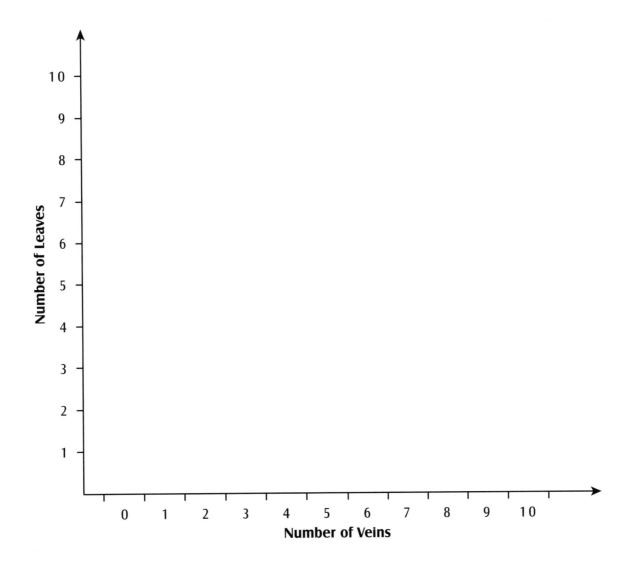

CHAPTER 5: FIRE AND ICE

Name _____

Date _____

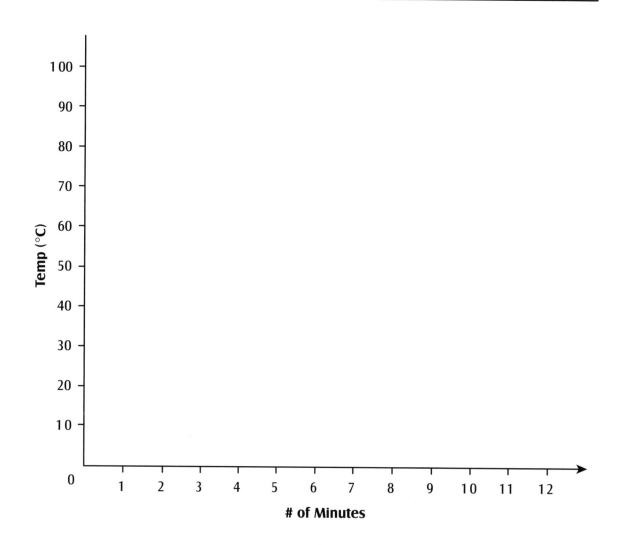

Glossary

Abacus

A manual computing device made up of a frame or two flat support pieces holding in place several parallel rods strung with an equal number of movable counters.

Absolute value

The numerical value or size of a quantity without regard to its sign.

Acute angle

An angle that measures less than 90°.

Acute triangle

A triangle *all* of whose angles are less than 90°.

Additive inverse

A number (a) added to its additive inverse (sign opposite) is 0, or **a + (−a) = 0**.

Algebra

A generalization of arithmetic in which letters of the alphabet represent numbers or a specified set of numbers related by operations that hold for all numbers in the set.

Altitude

The perpendicular distance measured from the base of a geometric figure to its opposite vertex or parallel side.

Analog clock

A face clock with as many as three dials to represent hours, minutes, and seconds.

Angle

The geometric figure formed by two rays (two lines extending from a common point).

Arc

A segment of a curve (usually a circle).

Area

The measure of a section or a region of a plane, measured in square units.

Arithmetic

The mathematics of integers under a binary operation(s).

Arithmetic progression

A sequence of numbers in which each term after the first is generated by adding a constant value (or "common difference") to each preceding term.

Average

The number (also known as the **arithmetic mean**) found by dividing the sum of a set of quantities by the number of those quantities in the set.

Bar graph

A discrete graph that uses the lengths of solid (rectangular) bars to represent quantities so as to allow for a comparison of data.

Base angles

The two equal angles of an isosceles triangle opposite its two congruent sides.

Binary operation

An operation—addition, subtraction, multiplication, or division—applied to two numbers to produce a third number.

Bisection

A division of a geometric figure into two equal parts.

Cartesian plane (or coordinate grid or Cartesian coordinate system)

A geometric construct wherein ordered pairs of numbers are represented by means of the rules of coordinate geometry.

Central angle

An angle with the center of a circle as its vertex and two radii as its sides.

Chord

A line segment connecting two points on a circle.

Circle

A planar, enclosed curve in which all of its points are equidistant from a given point (the center of the circle).

Circle graph

A graph that depicts how a whole is broken into parts (usually accompanied by a relative frequency, or percentage, per each part).

Circumference

The perimeter of a circle.

Combination

A group or arrangement of numbers, items, or events in which their order *does not matter.* (*See also* **permutation.**)

Common factor

Either of the two numbers (which, when multiplied, create a multiple) that are the same for two or more quantities.

Complementary angles

Two angles whose measures add up to 90°.

Composite number

An integer divisible by itself, by 1, *and* by at least one other integer. (*See also* **prime number.**)

Concentric circles

Like on an archery target, circles having a common center.

Congruent polygons

Two multisided figures whose sides and angles perfectly coincide.

Consecutive numbers

Numbers that follow each other in sequence without interruption.

Constant

An invariable quantity. (*See also* **variable.**)

Constant (linear) function

The line y = x, the 45° diagonal line passing through Quadrants I and III and the origin of the coordinate plane.

Corresponding angles

Given two parallel lines and a transversal (a line passing across both lines), the four pairs of angles in the same position from one parallel line to the other.

Cube

A regular rectangular solid with six congruent square faces.

Cylinder

A solid figure with two circular bases that are congruent and parallel.

Data

Numerical information sorted for analysis and used to reach a decision(s).

Decimal

A number containing a decimal point and derived from fraction form in which the denominator is some power of 10.

Deductive reasoning

Moving from generality (formula) to specifics (examples)—the outdated antithesis of the growing amount of "do-math-to-know-more-math" research (NCTM, 2000). (*See also* **inductive reasoning**.)

Denominator

In fraction form, the number *below* the line indicating the number of congruent smaller units into which a whole is being divided.

Diameter

One of the infinite number of chords that pass through a circle's center with the endpoints on the circle itself.

Dilation

An expansion or contraction of a geometric figure by a scale factor of "k," where k = a constant of proportionality.

Dimensional analysis

A series of steps designed to change fundamental measure from one type (e.g., miles per hour) to another type (e.g., feet per second).

Direct isometry

A transformation that not only preserves distance (*see also* **isometry**) but also preserves orientation or order.

Dot plot

A graph in which all the data is represented by points or dots.

Edge

The line of intersection of two surfaces of a solid.

Equiangular triangle

A triangle in which all three angles are of equal measure (*see also* **equilateral triangle**).

Equilateral triangle

A triangle in which all three sides are the same length (*see also* **equiangular triangle**).

Euler's Formula

Where V = the number of vertices, F = the number of faces, and E = the number of edges in any given polyhedron: $V + F = E + 2$.

Even number

Any number that is divisible by 2.

Exponent

A number or symbol placed in superscript position and to the right of another number or symbol to represent the power to which the latter (called the base) is to be raised.

Face

That part of a plane acting as a boundary for a given geometric solid.

Fraction

An indicated quotient of two quantities (*see also* **numerator**, **denominator**).

Function

A two-variable rule such that, for each value assumed by the first (the *independent* variable), there becomes a value determined for the second (the *dependent* variable).

Geometry

The mathematics of the properties and measurements of points, lines, angles, planes, and solids and how they relate to one another.

Glide reflection

The only transformation involving more than one step, it combines a reflection with a translation (or vice versa) along the direction of the mirror line (like footprints).

Great circle

The intersection of the Earth's surface with a plane passing through the center of the Earth.

Greatest Common Factor (GCF)

The greatest number that is a factor of two or more whole numbers.

Hexagon

A polygon with six sides.

Histogram

A continuous graph that uses the lengths of solid (rectangular) bars to represent how often the given data falls into particular ranges or intervals.

Horizontal line symmetry

What a two-dimensional figure has when folded in half with a horizontal line and its two halves match exactly.

Horizontal plane symmetry

What a three-dimensional solid has when folded in half with a horizontal plane and its two halves match exactly.

Hypotenuse

The side opposite the right angle in a right triangle and its longest side.

Hypothesis

A theory, or "calculated guess," which attempts to explain a set of facts and which, by extension, can be tested by further investigation.

Identity element

A number that combines with something else without changing it (0 is the additive identity element for $a + 0 = a$, and 1 is the multiplicative identity element for $a \times 1 = a$).

Image

An exact resemblance, or "double," of an original point or figure (the pre-image) when a transformation is performed on it.

Improper fraction

A fraction in which the numerator is greater than or equal to the denominator.

Indirect (opposite) isometry

A transformation that preserves distance (*see also* **isometry**) but also changes orientation or order (e.g., clockwise to counterclockwise).

Indirect measurement

A technique that uses proportions to find a measurement when direct measurement is impossible.

Inductive reasoning

Moving from specifics (numbers and observed patterns) to generalities that involve making conclusions (writing and testing formulas much like with the scientific method) based on those observations. (*See also* **deductive reasoning**.)

Inscribed angle

An angle in which the vertex lies directly on the circle and in which the sides are chords of the circle. The measure of an inscribed angle is equal to the measure of the intercepted arc (the subtended angle of the circle).

Inscribed square

A square drawn inside of a circle such that any of the square's vertices also represent one of the two endpoints of the radius of that circle.

Integer

A member of the set of whole numbers and their opposites.

Intercept The distance on either axis of the coordinate plane from the origin to the point at which a line or curve intersects that axis.

Inverse element

A number that combines with something else to produce an identity element.

Inverse proportion

When one quantity increases by a certain factor, a second quantity decreases by that same factor, or vice versa. (*See also* **direct proportion**.)

Isometry

A transformation that preserves distance.

Isosceles trapezoid

A trapezoid in which the base angles are equal (and thus also with congruent legs).

Isosceles triangle

A triangle that has two congruent sides (called *legs*).

Isotherm

A region drawn on a weather map to indicate various points of equal temperature.

Latitude

The angular distance (measured in degrees) north or south of the equator.

Law of Large Numbers

Empirical (experimental) probability begins to approach the value of theoretical (predictive) probability the longer a particular experiment is repeated.

Least Common Multiple (LCM)

The smallest positive integer that is a multiple of two or more quantities.

Leg

1. Either of the two congruent sides of an isosceles triangle; **2.** Either of the sides of a right triangle which is not the hypotenuse; **3.** Either of the nonparallel opposite sides of a trapezoid.

Line

A straight path of points with no endpoints.

Linear equation

An algebraic equation, $ax + by = c$, in which the highest-degree term between the two variables x and y is of the first degree.

Line graph

A graph comprising a series of connected line segments whose endpoints represent data.

Line segment

A measurable part of a line, comprising two endpoints and all of the points in between.

Longitude

The angular distance (measured in degrees) east or west of the prime meridian.

Matrix

A rectangular array of numerical or algebraic quantities in "m-by-n" format that is treated as an algebraic entity (m = # of *rows*, or "across" lines of elements; n = # of *columns*, or "up-and-down" lines of elements).

Mean

The sum of a set of numbers divided by how many numbers comprise that set.

Median

1. In geometry, a line segment drawn from one vertex of a triangle to the midpoint of the opposite side; **2.** In statistics, the number that falls in the exact middle of a set of data arranged from lowest to highest.

Midpoint

The point that divides a line segment into two congruent halves.

Mirror line

The line of reflection over which a pre-image becomes an image.

Mixed number

A number equal to the sum of an integer and a fraction.

Mode

The data item that appears the greatest number of times in a data set. (*Note:* A data set may have no mode, one mode, or more than one mode.)

Multiplicative inverse (or reciprocal)

A number (a) multiplied by its multiplicative inverse is 1, or $a \times \frac{1}{a} = 1$.

Natural number

A positive counting number: 1, 2, 3, . . .

Numerator

In fraction form, the number *above* the line representing *how many* of the parts of the whole represented by the bottom number (the denominator) one wishes to discuss.

Obtuse angle

An angle that measures greater than 90° but less than 180°.

Obtuse triangle

A triangle with one of its angles being obtuse.

Odd number

Any number that, when divided by 2, leaves a remainder of 1.

Orientation

The location or position of points relative to one another.

Parallel lines

Two coplanar lines keeping a constant equidistance apart and, thus, never intersecting.

Parallelogram

A quadrilateral with both pairs of its opposite sides congruent and parallel.

Percent

A term literally meaning "per hundred."

Perfect square

Any number that is the product of the same two whole-number factors.

Perimeter

The length of the closed curve bounding a plane area.

Permutation

A group or arrangement of numbers, items, or events in which their order *does* matter. (*See also* **combination**.)

Perpendicular bisector

A line or line segment that is perpendicular to *and* bisects the segment when drawn from its opposite vertex.

Perpendicular lines

Two lines that form right angles at their point of intersection.

Pictograph

A pictorial representation of data (e.g., in a particular graph of ethanol production, each corn stalk displayed might represent 1,000 bushels of corn).

Point

An abstract place in space that can be specified with a dot representation and, more times than not, a label.

Point of rotation (or turn center)

The point around which a point(s) is/are turned.

Polygon

A many-sided, closed figure bounded by *at least* three line segments.

Polyhedron

A many-faced solid bounded by polygons.

Population

The set of elements or data from which a statistical sample is taken. (*See also* **sample**.)

Pre-image

The original (given) point or figure prior to its transformation.

Prime factorization

A composite number written as a product of prime numbers.

Prime number

An integer divisible *only* by itself and by 1. (*See also* **composite number**.)

Prism

A polyhedron with at least two of its faces (called bases) congruent and parallel.

Probability

The ratio of desired outcomes of an event to possible outcomes, whose value **P** is always between 0 and 1, inclusive.

Proper fraction

A fraction in which the numerator is less than the denominator.

Proportion

A relation of equality between two ratios.

Pythagorean Theorem

In a right triangle, the square of the length of the hypotenuse is equal to the sum of the squares of its legs (or $c^2 = a^2 + b^2$).

Quadrant

One of the four sections the coordinate plane is divided into by the perpendicular x- and y-axes.

Quadrilateral

A four-sided geometric figure.

Radius

A segment with one endpoint on a circle and the other endpoint at the center of the circle (measuring half the length of the circle's diameter).

Range

The difference between the highest and lowest numbers in a set of data.

Ratio

A comparison of two quantities by division, usually in fraction form.

Ray

A half-line, extending straight out from an endpoint.

Rectangle

A parallelogram with its adjacent sides perpendicular to each other.

Rectangular solid

A prism whose bases are rectangles.

Reflection

A transformation in which a point(s) is/are "flipped" over a mirror line.

Region

An area; that is, a continuous part of a plane or of space.

Regular polygon

A polygon all of whose sides and angles are congruent.

Relatively-prime numbers

Numbers whose greatest common factor is 1.

Rhombus

An equilateral parallelogram.

Right angle

An angle that measures 90°.

Right trapezoid

A trapezoid with two adjacent right angles.

Right triangle

A triangle containing one right angle.

Rotation

The process of "turning" a point(s) around a given point (the point of rotation).

Rotational line symmetry

What a three-dimensional solid has if it rotates onto itself before turning 360° around a given line.

Rotational point symmetry

What a two-dimensional figure has if it rotates onto itself before turning 360° around a given point.

Sample

A subset of elements drawn from a certain population so that one can make inferences about the population from that sample.

Sample space

The list of all possible outcomes of an event.

Scalene triangle

A triangle all of whose sides are of different lengths.

Scientific method

Principles and procedures for identifying a problem, collecting data through observation and experiment, and forming and testing hypotheses.

Semicircle

A halfcircle as divided by a diameter.

Similar polygons

Two figures with matching angles that are congruent and matching sides that are proportional.

Slope of a line or line segment

Reveals how the value of y changes as the value of x changes. Given any two points, (x_1, y_1) and (x_2, y_2), the slope of the line of line segment through those two points = (change in y) ÷ (change in x) = $(y_2 - y_1) \div (x - x_1)$

Spectrogram

A graph or picture of a full distribution of colors.

Sphere

A three-dimensional solid (resembling a ball or globe) in which all points on the surface are equidistant from its center.

Square

An equilateral rectangle.

Square number

Any product of a number and itself.

Statistics

The collection, organization, and analysis of data.

Stem-and-leaf plot

A visual method of organizing data whereby the value of every piece of data is retained for quick analysis.

Straight angle

An angle that measures 180°, the result of two opposite rays sharing a common endpoint and forming a straight line.

Subtended arc

The piece of a circle opposite from and "chopped" by the sides of an angle.

Supplementary angles

Two angles whose measures add up to 180°.

Surface area

The measure of how much exposed area any three-dimensional object has, calculated by adding together the areas of all of its faces.

Tessellation

A pattern of shapes that is repeated over and over to cover some specified area.

Transformation

The mapping of a point(s) from one shape or place to another.

Translation

A transformation in which point(s) is/are moved a certain distance and direction by means of a "slide."

Trapezoid

A quadrilateral with two parallel sides.

Tree diagram

A visual mapping of the development of all possible outcomes of an event and sometimes drawn to help write the sample space.

Triangle

A three-sided polygon.

Triangular number

A natural number (written as the sum **1 + 2 + 3 + . . . + n** for some natural number n) such that the shape of an equilateral triangle can be formed by that number of points.

Trisection

A division of a geometric figure into three equal parts.

Variable

A quantity whose value changes. (*See also* **constant**.)

Venn Diagram

A pictorial representation using a rectangle and combinations of interlocking and/or separate circles. It is drawn in such a way as to represent operations found in set theory.

Vertex

The point of intersection of two sides of an angle, two adjacent sides of a polygon, or the converging edges of a polyhedron.

Vertex angle

The angle opposite the base of an isosceles triangle and having a different measure than either of the base angles.

Vertical line symmetry

What a two-dimensional figure has when folded in half with a vertical line and its two halves match exactly.

Vertical plane symmetry

What a three-dimensional solid has when folded in half with a vertical plane and its two halves match exactly.

Volume

The amount of space inside a solid or a prism, measured in cubic units.

Whole number

The set of natural numbers and zero.

References

Bartlett, J. (1968). *Familiar quotations*. (14th ed.). E. M. Beck (Ed.), Boston: Little, Brown.

Brown, S. I., & Walter, M. (1983). *The art of problem posing*. Hillsdale, NJ: Lawrence Erlbaum.

Great Source Education Group. (2000) *Algebra to go: A mathematics handbook*. Wilmington, MA: Author.

Great Source Education Group. (2000). *Math on call: A mathematical handbook*. Wilmington, MA: Author.

Gardner, H. (1993). *Multiple intelligences: The theory in practice*. New York: Basic Books.

Hart, D. (1994). *Authentic assessment: A handbook for educators*. Menlo Park, CA: Addison-Wesley.

Loomis, E. (1968). *The Pythagorean proposition*. Reston, VA: National Council of Teachers of Mathematics.

McClain, K. (1999, March). Reflecting on students' understanding of data. *Mathematics Teaching in the Middle School, 4*, 374–380.

McNamara, T. J. (2007). *Key concepts in mathematics: Strengthening standards practice in grades 6–12*. (2nd ed.). Thousand Oaks, CA: Corwin Press.

McNamara, T. J. (2003). *Key concepts in mathematics: Strengthening standards practice in grades 6–12*. Thousand Oaks, CA: Corwin Press.

National Council of Teachers of Mathematics. (2000). *Principles and standards for school mathematics*. Reston, VA: Author.

National Council of Teachers of Mathematics. (1991). *Professional standards for teaching mathematics*. Reston, VA: Author.

National Council of Teachers of Mathematics. (1980). *Sourcebook of application of school mathematics*. Reston, VA: Author.

National Council of Teachers of Mathematics. (1989). *Teaching and learning: A problem-solving focus*. Curcio, F. (Ed.). Reston, VA: Author.

Nelsen, R. B. (1993). *Proofs without words: Exercises in visual thinking*. Washington, DC: Mathematical Association of America.

Pedersen, J. & Pólya, G. (1984, June). On problems with solutions attainable in more than one way. *College Mathematics Journal, 15*, 218–228.

Pólya, G. (1957). *How to solve it: A new aspect of mathematical method*. (2nd ed.). Princeton, NJ: Princeton University Press.

Sandefur, J. T. (1985). Discrete mathematics: A unified approach. In C. Hirsch (Ed.), *The secondary school mathematics curriculum, 1995 yearbook of the National Council of Teachers of Mathematics*. Reston, VA: National Council of Teachers of Mathematics.

Schoenfeld, A. H. (1985). *Mathematical problem solving*. Orlando, FL: Academic Press.

The universal encyclopedia of mathematics. (1964). New York: Simon and Schuster.

Sobel, M. A., & Maletsky, E. A. (1988). *Teaching mathematics: A sourcebook of aids, activities, and strategies*. Englewood Cliffs, NJ: Prentice Hall.

Index